제4판

TOURISM ENGLISH FOR TRAVELING

관광여행영어

Limb, Joo-Hwan

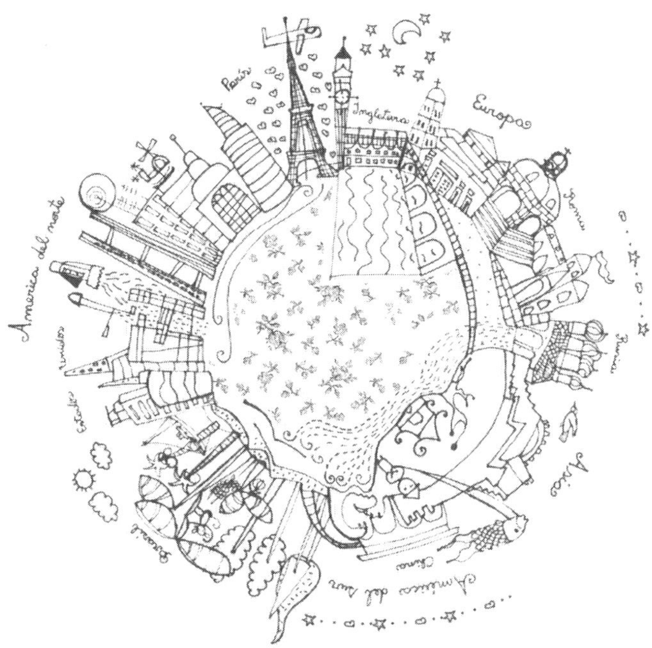

백산출판사

제4판을 내면서

관광이 생활의 필수재로서 전 세계인의 사랑을 받으며 하나의 사회제도로 자리 잡은 지 오래되었다. 현대인에게 관광은 생활의 필수 요건이라 해도 과언이 아니다. 제2차 세계대전 이후 서구사회에서부터 시작된 국제관광은 21세기에 이르는 오늘날까지 경제의 발전 그 이상으로 꾸준히 성장하고 있으며, 미래사회에서도 여전히 성장할 것으로 보여, 최고의 산업에 이를 것으로 전망하고 있다.

관광과 관광산업은 한국 경제의 발전과 함께하면서 오늘날 한국인에게 역시 생활의 일부분이 되었다. 우리나라에서는 1960년대부터 국가발전의 주요 전략사업으로 육성하기 시작하여, 1979년 인바운드 시장에서 연 100만 명을 초과달성하였으며, 1989년 해외여행 전면자율화가 시행된 후에는 아웃바운드에서도 100만 명을 초과하여 해마다 급속한 성장을 보여 왔다. 2014년에는 인바운드 1,400만 명, 아웃바운드 1,600만 명, 도합 3,000만 명을 달성하는 성과를 보였다. 급기야 2018년도에는 인바운드 1,530만 명, 아웃바운드 2,860만 명으로 도합 4,390만 명의 가히 국제관광의 전성시대를 눈앞에 두고 있다.

이와 같이 국제관광은 이제 국민 대다수의 생활의 일부로 자리 잡았을 뿐만 아니라, 국제 언어인 영어로 인하여 국경도, 언어장벽도 무너진 지 오래되었다. 따라서 영어는 단순한 외국어를 넘어 국제관광인에게는 자연스런 국제 통용어가 되었다. 영어를 못하면 개인도 국가도 고립되어 잠시도 살아갈 수 없는 시대가 되었다. 예를 들어 자국어를 고집하던 프랑스조차 이제는 국제어로 영어를 자연스레 사용하는 형편에 이르렀을 정도이다. 물론 발달된 ICT와 인공지능 덕분에 훌륭한 영어통역기나 번역기기가 출시되어 국제관광 초보자들에게 많이 활용되고 있긴 하다. 그러나 언어라는 문제는 사람의 정서가 교류되고 마음이 전달되는 문제이기 때문에 기기의 도움을 받는 것은 여전히 한계가 있다고 하겠다.

여러 외국인과 정서적으로 교류하고 자연스럽게 교감하기 위해서는 국제적인 영어에 익숙해지고 체화되는 수밖에 없다고 하겠다. 이에 본 교재를 통해서 영어 학습을 한다면 여행의 순간이나 장면이 자연스레 상기되도록 하여 각 장면의 영어에 익숙해질 수 있다. 이 책이 독자들의 사랑을 받아 지금까지 거듭하여 개정판을 내면서, 그간 부족했던 내용을 많이 보완하고 개정하게 되었다. 이에 제4판에서는 원어민 교재를 직접 참고하여 많이 보완 향상 시켰다. 책에는 Part Ⅰ에서 Hotel과 Airline 영어, Part Ⅱ에서는 전반적인 Tourism 영어, Part Ⅲ에서는 Articles on Tourism, Part Ⅳ에서는 Korea in Brief, Part Ⅴ에서는 기타부문을, 그리고 마지막 부록에서는 Proverbs를 실어 관광 전반에 대한 내용을 다루었다.

본 저자는 한국관광공사 재직 시에 호주, 미국 및 독일에 유학하여 관광전문과정을 수료하고, 내적으로는 관광업계의 간부, 호텔종사원, 관광통역사 양성과 외적으론 미주 지사장, 동남아 지사장, 해외유치단장 등 국내외적으로 관광영어와 더불어 생활해 왔으며, 대학에서는 관광학을 영어 중심으로 강의해 왔다. 그리고 지금도 여러 사회교육기관에서 여행 영어와 팝송을 강의하고 있다. 부디 이 책이 관광업계에 취업을 원하는 자, 관광업계 종사자, 관광계열 학도, 특히 관광통역안내사, 항공업계 및 관련업계의 자격시험과 국제관광에 나서는 사람들에게 큰 도움이 되길 바란다. 끝으로 이 책을 내면서 항상 열과 성을 다해준 백산출판사 진욱상 사장님과 편집부 여러분께 깊은 감사를 드린다.

2019. 4.
분당 자택에서
임 주 환

CONTENTS

Part I • Hotel & Airline English

Hotel English

Unit 01. Reservation Clerk ········· 17
Unit 02. Doorman ········· 20
Unit 03. Room Clerk ········· 21
Unit 04. Bellman ········· 25
Unit 05. Telephone Operator ········· 27
Unit 06. Information Clerk ········· 30
Unit 07. Mail Clerk ········· 33
Unit 08. Check Room Attendant ········· 35
Unit 09. Front Cashier ········· 37
Unit 10. Housekeeper ········· 39
Unit 11. Room Maid ········· 42
Unit 12. Laundry Clerk ········· 44
Unit 13. Receptionist ········· 46
Unit 14. Breakfast ········· 48
Unit 15. Luncheon ········· 50
Unit 16. Dinner ········· 52
Unit 17. Bar ········· 55

Unit 18. Room Service ························ 57

Airline English

Unit 01. Reservation ························ 60
1) Request reservation • 60
2) Traveling with children • 62
3) Transfer flight schedules • 63
4) Reconfirmation • 64
5) Canceling reservation • 65
Unit 02. Ticketing ························ 66
Unit 03. Checking in ························ 67
Unit 04. Security Check-In ························ 70
Unit 05. Pre-boarding Station ························ 70
Unit 06. Check-In Announcements ························ 71
1) Government formalities for departure • 71
2) Check-in • 71
3) Security check-in • 72
4) Final call security check-in • 72
5) Departure delayed • 72
6) Departure cancelled • 73
7) Boarding • 73
Unit 07. Passenger Boarding ························ 74
1) At the door • 74
2) In the cabin • 74

Unit 08. Seating Guide 77

1) Separated passenger • 77

2) Changing seats • 79

3) Wrong seats • 80

4) Double seating • 81

5) Luggage in the aisle • 81

6) Luggage in the seat • 83

7) Luggage in the overhead compartment • 83

Unit 09. Preparations for Take-off 84

1) Seat belt check • 84

2) Tray table / Seat back • 85

3) Newspaper service • 85

4) Delay in departure • 86

Unit 10. Before Take-off Announcement 86

1) Boarding • 86

2) Takeoff delayed • 87

3) Welcome • 87

4) Safety demonstration • 89

5) Takeoff • 90

6) Restriction on using electronic service • 90

Unit 11. Earphone and Travel Service 91

1) Hot towel service • 91

2) Earphone service • 92

Unit 12. Meal and Beverage Service 92

1) Beverage service • 92

2) Meal service • 94

3) Wine service • 96

4) Coffee and Tea service • 97

5) Meal tray pick-up • 97

Unit 13. In-Flight Music and Movie ········· 98

Unit 14. Service and Comfort ········· 101

Unit 15. Sick Passenger Handling ········· 103

Unit 16. In-Flight Sales ········· 105

Unit 17. CIQ Information ········· 108

Unit 18. Destination City Information ········· 109

Unit 19. Landing and Deplaning ········· 111

Unit 20. En-Route Announcements ········· 113

1) Service plan • 113

2) Meal and beverage • 113

3) In-Flight movie • 113

4) Turbulence • 114

5) In-Flight duty-free sales • 114

6) Flying over scenic spots • 114

7) Document • 115

8) Headphone collection • 116

9) Destination approaching • 117

Unit 21. Landing ········· 118

Unit 22. Farewell ········· 118

Unit 23. Deplaning ········· 119

Unit 24. Immigration ········· 119

Unit 25. Baggage Claim ········· 121

Unit 26. Customs ········· 123

Unit 27. Money Exchange Counter ······ 125
Unit 28. Check-Out Announcements ······ 127
1) Arrival • 127
2) Paging • 127
3) Arrival delayed • 127
4) Arrival cancelled • 128
5) Diverted flight • 128
6) Lost & found • 129

Part II • Tourism English

Unit 01. At The Travel Bureau ······ 133
Unit 02. Informations For Tour ······ 135
Unit 03. On The Street ······ 137
Unit 04. On The Train ······ 139
Unit 05. At The Bank ······ 142
Unit 06. At The Travel Agency ······ 145
Unit 07. At The Department Store ······ 146
Unit 08. Talking About Sightseeing ······ 148
Unit 09. Downtown Seoul ······ 166
Unit 10. Meeting Service ······ 171
Unit 11. Reservation For Breakfast ······ 176
Unit 12. Food Service ······ 178

Unit 13. Renting A Car ········· 181
Unit 14. Phone Call ········· 186
Unit 15. Going To A Restaurant ········· 188
Unit 16. Public Transportation ········· 189
Unit 17. Invitations ········· 190
Unit 18. Asking Directions ········· 192
Unit 19. At The Post Office ········· 193
Unit 20. At The Pharmacy ········· 194

Part III • Articles on Tourism

Unit 01. Tourism Today ········· 199
Unit 02. Tourism Defined ········· 200
1) Tourism defined • 200
2) Tourism more broadly defined • 205
Unit 03. Domestic Tourism ········· 207
1) Domestic tourism • 207
2) Local tourism • 208
Unit 04. International Tourism ········· 209
- Developing countries • 209
- Balance of trade • 210
Unit 05. International Government Organizations ········· 211
- UN World Tourism Organization

(UNWTO) • 211
- International Civil Aviation Organization (ICAO) • 213
- International Air Transport Association (IATA) • 213
- Organization for Economic Cooperation and Development (OECD) • 215
- Organization of American States (OAS) • 215
- Pacific Asia Travel Association (PATA) • 216
- American Society of Travel Agents (ASTA) • 216
- Other Organizations • 216

Part IV • Korea in Brief

Unit 01. History 221
- Dangun and the Founding Myth of Korea • 222
Unit 02. Land 224
Unit 03. Climate 225
Unit 04. Religion 226
Unit 05. Language 227
Unit 06. Seoul 228
Unit 07. Gyeongju 229

Part V • Others

Unit 01. Job Interviewing ······ 235
Unit 02. Self Introduction (Autobiography) ······ 239
1) Self-Introduction • 241
2) Family Background • 241
3) Motto (Basic principle of my life) • 242
4) Personality • 242
5) Interests and Hobbies • 242
6) My Goals in Life • 242
Unit 03. Personal History (Resume) ······ 243
Unit 04. Hospitality Personnel Guideline ······ 244
1) Smile • 244
2) A Guide to Hospitality Industry • 245
3) Personal Services as an Escort • 246
- Do • 246 - Don't • 247
4) What does PLEASE mean? • 247

|부 록| Proverbs ······ 249

Part
I

Hotel & Airline English

Hotel English

Unit • 01 Reservation Clerk

Dialog 1

A : Guest, B : Clerk

A : Hello, is this Korea Hotel?

B : Yes, may I help you, sir?

A : Yes, please. Can I put up at your hotel tonight?

B : Certainly, sir.
What kind of room would you like to have?

A : A double room with bath, please.

B : Very good, sir.

A : I'll take it.

B : Thank you, sir. May I have your name, please?

A : Mr. and Mrs. Bush. We are from Los Angeles.

B : I see. How long are you going to stay here?

A : About a fortnight.

B : Thanks for calling.

Dialog 2

A : Guest, B : Clerk

A : Hello, this is Mr. Regan.
Is this Hilton Hotel?

B : Yes, sir. Can I help you?

A : I'd like to get a room.

B : Thank you very much.
What kind of room would you like, sir?

A : A single room with bath, please.

B : Very good, sir. We have a nice room available.

A : I'll take it. I'll be there shortly.

B : Yes, sir. We shall be waiting for you.

Dialog 3

A : Clerk, B : Guest

A : Reservation desk. Miss Kim speaking.
May I help you?

B : This is C & G Corporation in Seoul.
I'd like to make a reservation.

A : May I have your name and phone number, please?

B : Thomas Johnson. 502-1234.

A : What kind of room would you like, sir?

B : A double room with bath, please.

A : How long are you going to stay here, sir?

B : I want to stay from May 1st through May 3rd.

A : Thank you for calling. We'll be waiting for you.

Dialog 4

A : Clerk, B : Guest

A : Good morning, this is reservation, Ritz-Carlton.
May I help you?

B : Yes, this is Mr. Johnson.
I have just arrived at the airport.
Do you have a single for tonight and tomorrow night?

A : Yes, sir. We have a single room with bath.

B : What is the room rate?

A : Twenty dollars per night.
The government tax and service charges will be added to this rate.

B : What are added?

A : The tax and service charges.

B : How much is it?

A : About 20%.

B : Very good, I'll take it.
My name is Mr. William H. Johnson from New York.
I'll be at the hotel by six o'clock.

Unit 02 Doorman

Dialog 1

A : Doorman, B : Guest

A : Good morning, sir.
May I help you with your baggage?

B : No, it's all right. It's not heavy.
So, I'll carry it by myself. Where can I register?

A : You can register at the front desk over there to your right.

B : Thank you.

A : Please watch out of the revolving door.
The inside door is automatic.

B : Thank you.

Dialog 2

A : Doorman, B : Guest

A : Good morning. sir.
Are you leaving today?

B : Yes, I'm going to take the flight at one o'clock.

A : Are you? It's ten past eleven now.
I think you'd better hurry.

B : I have a black bag in front of the hotel room.

Could you bring it to me?

A : Yes, sir. I'll load this baggage in the trunk.

Dialog 3

A : Doorman, B : Guest

A : Good morning. May I help you, sir?

B : Yes. Can you call my car, please?

A : Yes, what's the number?

B : 2211.

A : Wait a minute, please. I'll call it right away.

Unit • 03 Room Clerk

Dialog 1

A : Room Clerk, B : Guest

A : Good evening, sir. May I help you?

B : Good evening. I have a reservation here.

A : May I have your name, please?

B : Thomas Brown.

A : Oh, yes. We have your reservation.

A single room with bath, room 1825.

B : That's fine.

A : Would you fill out this form, please?

B : Here you are.

A : I hope you enjoy your stay here.

B : Thanks a lot.

Dialog 2

A : Room Clerk, B : Guest

A : Good evening, sir. May I help you?

B : Yes, please. Do you have a room?

A : Yes, we do. A double or a single?

B : A single.

A : How long will you be staying, sir?

B : Just for tonight. I'm going to Gyeongju tomorrow.

A : Very well, sir. Would you please register?

B : Here you are.

A : And the bellman will show you to your room. Have a nice day.

B : Thanks a lot.

Dialog 3

A : Room Clerk, B : Guest

A : May I have your name, sir?

B : My name is Thomas Brown.

A : Just a moment, please.
Yes, that's right. We have your reservation.
How long are you staying, sir?

B : I'm staying for two nights.
What's the rate of a single room with bath per day?

A : We have a single room with bath for 170 dollars per day.

B : That'll be fine. And I want a quiet room.

A : Of course you can have a very quiet room.
It's on the 17th floor with a nice view.
Will you register here, please?

B : All right.

A : Here's your key. Your room number is 2300.
The porter will carry your baggage.

B : Thank you.

Dialog 4

A : Room Clerk, B : Guest

A : Good morning, sir. Welcome to Hilton Hotel.
May I help you?

B : I want a room for the next ten days.
Do you have one?

A : Do you have a reservation, sir?

B : No, I don't.

A : Just a moment, sir.

I'll check to see if we have a room available.

Would a studio twin room be all right, sir?

B : What's studio twin room?

A : It's a twin room with a studio bed that can fold up into a sofa.

B : That will be fine.

A : We do not have any room available for a full ten nights.

[We don't have any rooms available for such a period]

Would you mind changing room in the middle of your stay?

B : No, it's all right with me.

A : Thank you, sir. Would you please register here?

Please be sure to fill in everything.

B : All right. Here you are.

A : Thank you, sir.

A bellboy will show you to your room.

Unit 04 Bellman

Dialog 1

A : Bellman, B : Guest

A : Your baggage, please?

B : This bag, suit case, and that golf club bag there.

A : Any other baggage coming, sir?

B : Yes, I've got two more pieces coming.

A : Now, this way, please.

B : This room looks all right.

A : Thank you, sir. Built-in closet here and bathroom over there.

B : I want to send a cable.
Will you get me a cable form?

A : All stationery is in this desk drawer, sir.

B : That's fine.

A : Anything else(I can do), sir?

B : No, I guess that's all.

Dialog 2

A : Bellman, B : Guest

A : There is a beauty parlor and barber's in the first basement, sir.

B : How late do they stay open?

A : Until 8 o'clock, sir.

B : Thanks. That gives us plenty of time.

A : Here is your room, sir.

Closet with clothes hangers here, and here is the bathroom.

Stationery, room service menu and a brochure giving all the services of the hotel are in this desk.

Light switches here and thermostat.

B : Thank you.

Dialog 3

A : Bellman, B : Guest

A : This is where we get off. Down this way, please.

B : This is a nice room, isn't it?

I think we ought to be comfortable here.

B : This is for you.

A : I'm sorry, but, no tipping is our pride.

If you need anything, just call the desk.

Dialog 4

A : Bellman, B : Guest, C : Clerk

C : (Calls for a bellman) Show Mr. Brown to room 705.

A : Yes, sir. Are these your bags?

B : Yes, they are.

A : This way please.
Here we are 705. (Bellman opens the door.)
Here's the light switch for the bathroom, the radio and the air conditioning.
The TV set, as you can see here, and the switch is on the right side of the set.

B : Is it a sunny room?

A : No, sir. The sun never visits, but it commands a fine view of the river.

Unit · 05 Telephone Operator

Dialog 1

A : Telephone Operator, B : Guest

A : Good evening. This is operator speaking, sir.

B : Is this the operator?
This is Wilson in room 1614 speaking.

A : What can I do for you, Mr. Wilson?

B : Can you give me a morning call at 7 : 30?

A : Yes, sir. Mr. Wilson in room 1614, morning call at

7 : 30.

(…)

B : Wilson speaking.

A : Good morning. Mr. Wilson It is 7 : 30 now.

Dialog 2

A : Telephone Operator, B : Guest

A : Good morning. Operator.

B : Hello? Could you get me 502-9955, please.

A : Yes, sir. One moment, please.

B : Shall I hold the line or hang up?

A : Please hold the line....

I'm sorry, sir, but your party doesn't answer.

B : Well, never mind. I'll try again later.

Dialog 3

A : Guest, B : Operator

A : Operator?

I'd like to make an overseas call to New York.

B : Is it a person-to-person call, sir?

A : Yes. The party I want to call is Mr. Philip Dawson.

The number is 544-8236.

B : Mr. Philip Dawson, New York 544-8236?

A : Yes, that's right.

B : I t may take about fifteen minutes.
Will you be in your room, sir?

A : I'd like to take the call in the main dining room.

B : Very well, sir.
Please tell the head waiter that you are expecting a call.

Dialog 4

A : Operator, B : Guest

A : Operator. Prince Hotel, May I help you?

B : I want to speak to Mr. Custer, room 568, please.

A : Room 568? One moment please.
(The operator connects this call to 568)

Dialog 5

A : Operator, B : Guest

A : Operator, Prince Hotel, can I help you?

B : How can I call this phone number Seoul 702-8236?

A : Please dial zero first and then the number you want.

B : I see, thanks.

Dialog 6

A : Operator,　B : Guest

A : Prince Hotel operator, may I help you?

B : This is Woods, room 725.
Would you wake me up at six thirty tomorrow morning, please?

A : Mr. Wood, room 725, six thirty, call tomorrow morning?

B : Yes, please.

A : Very well, sir. Good night.

Unit 06 Information Clerk

Dialog 1

A : Guest,　B : Clerk

A : May I have some information on the night club?

B : Yes, sir.

A : Can you describe it in general?

B : Yes, it is located in the basement and open from 7 p.m. till 2 in the morning.
You can enjoy delightful music.

A : What time did you say the night club is closed?

B : It's closed at two o'clock in the morning, sir.

A : That's good. Can you make a reservation right now?

B : Yes, sir.

Dialog 2

A : Guest, B : Clerk

A : I heard that the Korean Folk Village is famous. How can I get there?

B : We have a shuttle bus going there, but it would be difficult for a foreigner to take it.

B : I would like to suggest that you either rent a car or use a tour bus of a travel agency.

A : It sounds very interesting. Can you reserve a cab immediately?

B : Certainly, sir. What time will you leave, sir?

A : It's 9 : 40 now. I would like to leave at ten.

B : Fine. Please come back at ten.

A : I see. It is very kind of you.

Dialog 3

A : Guest, B : Clerk

A : Can you recommend some place for our dinner?

B : Why don't you have your dinner at the Korean

Restaurant on the 7th floor.

A : Should I make a reservation?

B : Yes, sir. I think you had better make a reservation.

A : Will you put me on the reservation list?

B : Yes, sir. May I have your name, please?

A : My name is Thomas Brown.

Dialog 4

A : Guest, B : Clerk

A : When is check out time?

B : Check out time is 12 : 00 noon, sir.

A : What are the extra room charge?

B : If you check in before 05 : 00 a.m., there is one day's charge.

If you check in from 05 : 00 a.m. until 11 : 00 a.m., there's a 30% of one day's charge.

A : Do you offer any room service?

B : Yes, sir. Room service is available from 07 : 00 a.m. until 10 : 00 p.m. Just dial 3 for room service.

A : Is there a service charge for room service?

B : Yes, sir. A 10% service charge.

A : What's your laundry service hours?

B : If your laundry is received before 10 : 00 a.m., we

deliver it by 10 : 00 p.m. the same day. If you bring it before 3 : 00 p.m., we will get it back by noon the next day.

A : Who shall I call?

B : Please call the room maid.

A : Does she handle the dry cleaning and pressing?

B : Yes, sir.

A : Who do I call for morning call, please?

B : Please call the switch board (dial 9, please).

Unit · 07 Mail Clerk

Dialog 1

A : Guest, B : Clerk

A : What is the postal charge for this letter?
It is for the U.S.A.

B : It seems to be heavy. Let me weigh it first.
It is 18 grams.
The basic charge for the American area is 2,500 won.
It costs 2,500 won from 10 grams up to 20 grams, sir.

A : Please give me 2,500 won worth of stamps.

B : Sir. If you will give the postal charge and letter to me, I'll be glad to mail it for you. I stop by the post office twice a day.

Dialog 2

A : Guest, B : Clerk

A : Is there any mail for me? Room 705.

B : How are you, Mr, Smith.
We do not have any mail for you, sir.

A : I am supposed to have important document.
What is your mail delivery time?

B : Ten o'clock a.m. and three p.m. twice a day, sir.

Dialog 3

A : Guest, B : Clerk

A : Any mail for me?

B : We have just received letters. Let me check it.

A : I'm waiting for letters, you know.

B : Here they are.

A : Thanks a lot.

Dialog 4

A : Guest, B : Clerk

A : Would you give this message to Mrs, Limb?

B : Certainly. What's her room number, please?

A : I don't remember.
but I think she is on the fifth floor.

B : That's all right. I'll look it up.
How do you spell her name?

A : L.I.M.B. LIMB

B : Oh, yes, here it is. Room 502.
I'll see that she gets the message.

Unit • 08 Check Room Attemdant

Dialog 1

A : Checkroom attendant, B : Guest

A : How are you, sir? Are you leaving today?

B : Yes, I am leaving today.
I'd like to have this baggage kept here for a while.

A : Certainly, sir. When will you want it back, sir?

B : The plane will depart at 7 o'clock. As you know, the check-out time is 12 noon.

A : You are right, sir. If you should stay in your room till then, you would have to pay extra charge, sir.

B : I still have something to do.
I'll be back by 4 o'clock.

A : I see. Here is your baggage ticket, sir.

Dialog 2

A : Checkroom attendant, B : Guest

A : May I help you, sir?

B : Yes. I lost my baggage ticket.

A : That is a problem.
Can you remember the checking date?

B : It was on March 5th, the day I went down to Busan.

A : I hope your baggage is safe. Let's see the list.
May I have your name, please?

B : My name is Reed. I stayed in room 905.

A : Here it is. Fortunately, your baggage was not yet claimed.

Dialog 3

A : Checkroom attendant, B : Guest

B : One black travel bag and one case containing sample.
The case is this big, you know.

A : You seem to be the owner according to what you have said.
Could you identify yourself?

B : Yes, I will. Here is my passport.
You can believe that I am Reed.

A : Thank you. Wait a minute, sir.
First, I have to report it to my supervisor and follow his direction, sir.
Sorry to have kept you waiting, sir.
We have no doubt the baggage belongs to you.
It was just a procedure for safe handling, sir.
I hope you don't mind.

Unit 09 Front Cashier

Dialog 1

A : Cashier, B : Guest

A : May I help you?

B : Yes, I'd like to pay my account, room 5525.

A : Certainly, sir. I won't keep you one moment....
This is the total, sir, four hundred thousand won.

B : I'd like to have this charged to my account.

I've been a guest at your hotel on many occasions, and I've established credit arrangements with you.

A : Yes, sir. Will you sign the account, while I take down name and address?
Thank you, sir.

B : Thanks. Good-bye.

A : Good-bye, sir.

Dialog 2

A : Guest, B : Cashier

A : I am Baker in room 905. I am checking out today. Will you make out my bill?

B : Wait a moment, sir. It comes to a total of 258,500 won, sir.

A : Here you are.

B : Here is your change, 1,500 won, sir.

A : That is for you, though it is a small amount.
I don't need it, anyway.

B : Thank you. Here is your receipt, sir.

A : Thank you. I have enjoyed my stay here. Good-bye.

B : Good bye, sir. Please come again.

Dialog 3

A : Guest, B : Cashier

A : Yes, we are checking out.
We have to catch a plane at 12 : 30.
How much is our bill?

B : Just a moment, sir. Here it is, sir.
Fifty three thousand two hundred twenty five won.

A : I don't have that much won on me.
I'll have to give you part of it in dollars.
Let's see, here is one hundred dollars and ten thousand won. Will that do?

B : Yes, sir. Here is your change.
I hope you enjoyed your stay.
Please come again.

Unit・10 Housekeeper

Dialog 1

A : Clerk, B : Guest

A : This is frontdesk Kim speaking. Can I help you, sir?

B : This is Martin, room 707.
The room is not warm enough.

I am worried I might catch a cold.

A : There is a heating controller on the wall.
Is it properly adjusted?

B : I know how to handle the controller.
It is still cold though I adjusted it to highest.

A : Our engineer will be there within five minutes, sir.

Dialog 2

A : Clerk, B : Guest

B : This is room 1117. I have only five hangers.
Can you send some more hangers.

A : Certainly. Are you in room 1117?
Would three more hangers do?

B : Please send two more hangers and two more blankets.

A : I understand, sir. We will send additionally 2 hangers and 2 blankets to room 1117 right away.

Dialog 3

A : Clerk, B : Guest

B : This is Mrs. Baker who stayed in room 1711 of your hotel.
I am making a phone call from the airport now.

A : How are you Mrs, Baker? Aren't you calling because of the lost ring in room 1711?

B : Yes. Have you found it?

A : Yes, the room maid brought it.
You left it on the dresser.
We are keeping it at the lost and found section, ma'am.

Dialog 4

A : Clerk, B : Guest

A : This is frontdesk Kim speaking. May I help you?

B : Yes, I'll be out for half an hour.
I expect Mr. Thomas to come while I'm out.
Let him in and have him wait.

A : I'm sorry, sir.
We cannot let someone else into your room.
Would you like me to have him wait in the lobby on the first floor?

B : Yes. I think so.
Also, would you fix the desk lamp in my room?
It seems to be little dim.

A : Yes, sir. I'll have it taken care of right away.
Is there anything else?

B : No, that's all.

But try to have it done before I'm back.

A : Yes, sir.

Unit 11 Room Maid

Dialog 1

A : Guest, B : Room maid

A : I'm Sorry to have called you.

Can you bring some water in the water pitcher?

B : Oh, my goodness! I forgot to fill the water pitcher.

A : No, it was full, but I drank it all as I was very thirsty.

B : I see. I will bring it to you in a moment.

A : Would you go out of your way to bring me some ice water instead of hot water?

B : Yes, sir.

Dialog 2

A : Guest, B : Room maid

B : Are you leaving today?

A : Yes, I appreciate you special care during my stay

here.

B : You have lots of things to pack up. May I help you?

A : Thank you. I have to count on your help even at my leaving time.

B : Was there anything uncomfortable during your stay?

A : I really enjoyed my stay. If I have another chance to visit Korea, I will be pleased to make arrangements for my stay in your hotel.

Dialog 3

A : Guest, B : Room maid

A : Who is it?

B : Room maid. Good morning, sir.

A : Good morning. Do you want anything?

B : If you don't mind.
I would like to clean the room now.

A : Can you fix the room right now?

B : It will take about 15 minutes, sir.

A : You do a nice job, don't you?

Dialog 4

A : Room Maid, B : Guest

A : Good morning, this is the maid.

B : Good morning, will you come to room 705 please? I have some laundry and dry cleaning.

A : Yes, sir.

B : These things are for the laundry, and these are for dry cleaning.

A : Our valet has one or two hour quick service and a regular service.
Would you like to have them back in a hurry?

B : No, not particularly. I will take the regular service. Two suits for dry cleaning. five pairs of shorts and undershirts, and three white shirts.

A : All right, sir. Please sign here.

B : Okay.

A : Thank you, sir.

Unit 12 Laundry Clerk

Dialog 1

A : Guest, B : Clerk

A : I have to go to a party in this suit tonight.
Can you make it by then?

B : I think this should be dry-cleaned.
When do you want it to be delivered?

A : By six o'clock this evening.

B : You can get it by then, sir.

A : By the way, ask them to take this stain off, please.

B : Is this grease?

A : It might be fruit stain or something.
I don't know exactly.

B : Whatever it is. I'll ask them to remove it completely.

Dialog 2

A : Guest, B : Clerk

B : Laundry service, I have brought your laundry, sir.

A : Come in.

B : Yes, I believe you will be satisfied with them.
Would you check the laundry, please?

B : Here is the laundry slip you signed yesterday.

A : I believe it's correct. Yes, it's correct.

B : Thank you. Here is your laundry bill, sir.

A : Should I pay in cash?

B : As you like, sir. You can pay in cash or sign for it so that you can pay later when you check out, sir.

Dialog 3

A : Guest, B : Clerk

A : When can I get it back, if I send out laundry today?

B : Are you in a hurry?

A : No, not especially, but....

B : Usually you can get it back on the following day. But, if rushed, you can get it in the evening. There is an extra charge, though.

A : There is no rush. Let me have the laundry slip.

B : Here it is.

A : Good. You wait here as it won't take me long to fill out.

B : Certainly.

Unit 13 Receptionist

Dialog 1

A : Receptionist, B : Guest

A : Good evening, sir. Did you make a reservation, sir?

B : I am Baker, and this is my wife.
We reserved a table this morning.

A : This way, please.

B : It's a marvelous restaurant.
I think you have a lot of guests.

A : Thank you for your compliment, sir.
Here is your table, sir.

Dialog 2

A : Receptionist, B : Guest

A : Good evening. May I help you, sir?

B : Do you have a table for two?

A : You don't have a reservation, do you?

B : No.

A : We don't have any vacant tables.
Do you mind if you have to share a table, sir?

B : No, we don't.

Dialog 3

A : Receptionist, B : Guest

A : Good evening, sir? May I help you?

B : We have a reservation here. My name is Dean Martin.
A table for seven, please.

A : Would you follow me? Would you take those seats?

B : Fine. This table is O.K.

A : I hope you enjoy your dinner.

Unit 14 Breakfast

Dialog 1

A : Waiter, B : Guest

A : May I take your order, ma'am?

B : Yes. I'll have tomato juice, shredded wheat, and bacon and eggs.

A : Which would you prefer, tea or coffee?

B : Tea with milk, please.

A : How do you want your eggs?

B : Turned over, please.

A : Very well, ma'am.

B : Please rush my order.
I have to be at the airport by eight thirty.

A : Certainly, ma'am.
I would appreciate it if you would pay for your breakfast in cash.
That way, I won't have to bill you again.

Dialog 2

A : Waiter, B : Guest

A : Good morning, sir. Here is the menu, sir.
Would you like to have coffee first?

B : Now let me see.... I'll have coffee, toast, a small glass of fresh orange juice, and ham and eggs.

A : Very well.
Would you like to have some cereal ma'am?

B : Oh, yes, I would. Bring me corn flakes with raisins.

A : Yes, ma'am.
How would you like your toast, dark or light?

B : I want my toast dark.
Also, please bring me some marmalade.

A : Surely.

Dialog 3

A : Waiter, B : Guest

A : Good morning, sir. Some fruit?

B : What have you got this morning?

A : Assorted fresh fruit and some stewed prunes and figs.

B : Stewed figs?
Give me that and a glass of tomato juice.

A : Any cereal, sir?

B : Yes, a dish of cream of wheat.
I like to have my coffee now, too.

A : Egg or something?

B : I'd like two eggs and coffee.

A : Boiled or fried?

B : Fried.

A : Sunny-side up or turned over?

B : Turned over, please. I want them hot please.

Unit · 15 Luncheon

Dialog 1

A : Waiter, B : Guest

A : Would you care for cocktail?

B : One Martini, one Screw drives and two Gin Tonics, please.

A : Would you like to order now, sir?

B : Yes. one Lobster, one Scallop, one Filet Mignon, and one Sirloin Steak, please.

A : How would you like your steak, sir?

B : Medium rare, please.

A : Would you care for anything else?

B : Yes, I'd like some coffee, please.

A : Did you enjoy your food?

B : Yes, I enjoyed it very much.

A : Are you through, sir.

B : Yes, I'm done.

Dialog 2

A : Waiter, B : Guest

A : What would you like to order, sir?

B : I want some spaghetti.

A : I'm sorry, spaghetti is not on the menu.

B : Can you make some for me?

A : Just a moment, please.
I'll ask it. Yes, we can make some for you.
It will take about 15 minutes. All right. sir?

B : That's all right.

A : What kind of sauce do you like?

B : Tomato sauce, please. Bring me a salad, too.

A : What kind of salad dressing, sir?

B : Thousand dressing, please.

Dialog 3

A : Waiter, B : Guest

A : Are you ready to order now?

B : I guess so. I just want something light.
Do you have hamburgers?

A : Yes, Miss.

B : Good. Bring me a hamburger but hold the onions.

Dialog 4

A : Waiter, B : Guest

A : May I help you, sir?

B : Yes, I think I'll have roast beef.

A : Will you have soup or juice?

B : I think I'd like tomato juice.

A : Can I get you anything else?

B : Tea with milk, please.

Unit 16 Dinner

Dialog 1

A : Guest, B : Waiter

A : What's good on the menu tonight?

B : We are selling a lot of flounder tonight.
We have it baked or broiled.

A : I'm not too strong on fish.
I'll just have a medium rare steak.

B : Yes, sir.

Would you like baked potato or French fries?

A : Baked potato with sour cream, French dressing on my salad.

B : Yes, sir.

Dialog 2

A : Guest, B : Waiter

A : What kind of soup do you have?

B : We have potato, onion gratin soup, and clam chowder.

A : Clam chowder for us, please.

B : What would you like to drink?

A : We'll have beer. Two bottles, please.

B : And what would you like for dessert?

A : Do you have ice cream?

B : Yes, we have Banana, Chocolate, and Peach.

A : Banana, please.

B : Will that be all? Thank you, sir.

A : Check, please!

B : Thank you, sir.

A : Shall I pay here?

B : Please pay at the cashier.

A : O.K. Thank you.

Dialog 3

A : Assistant Manager, B : Guest

A : Did you enjoy your dinner?

B : Oh, very much. Excellent. By the way, we have here one "Happy Birthday and One Anniversary" to celebrate. How much do you charge for the celebration service?

A : Well, we charge you five dollars per person.
So, that will be 35 dollars in your party.
Also we serve you with Fresh Pineapple from Hawaii.

A : Now we're gonna sing "Happy Birthday and Happy Anniversary" to you.
Everybody, clap hands, please. Now here we go!

B : Thank you so much for the beautiful party.

Dialog 4

A : Guest, B : Waiter

A : Is there a specialty of the house?

B : Yes, ma'am. It‘s "Bulgogi."

A : What is it?

B : It's barbecued beef, ma'am, prepared Korean style.

A : Do you serve it with rice?

B : Yes, ma'am. We also serve "Kimchi" with it.

Unit 17 Bar

Dialog 1

A : Guest, B : Cocktail Waitress

A : Ms, please show me the wine list.

B : Very well, sir. Here you are, sir.

A : Thank you. Please bring me a martini.

B : Yes, sir. Would you like it dry?

A : Yes, extra dry, please.

B : Very well sir.

Dialog 2

A : Guest, B : Cocktail Waitress, C : Guest

B : What would you like to drink, sir?

A : Give me Tom Collins.

B : Very good, sir. With gin, or with vodka?

A : Please make it with gin.

B : Yes, sir.

C : Give me Scotch.

B : What brand?

C : White Horse, double.

B : Soda or water?

C : Just plain water with plenty of ice.

B : Have some potato chips.

C : Good. Give me another. What's that bottle over there? Let me see it. Do you have a match?

B : Yes, sir.

C : You are pretty well stocked here.

B : Right, sir.

Dialog 3

A : Guest, B : Cocktail Waitress

A : What does "Scotch on the rocks" mean?

B : "Rocks" means ice.
So it means straight Scotch with ice and no mixer.

A : I see. Are other things ordered that way, too?

B : Sure do. Bourbon on the rocks.
Gin on the rocks. Martini on the rocks.
And Vermouth on the rocks.
There are lots of possibilities.

A : If you don't want anything in your liquor, what should you ask for?

B : Just say, "I'll have straight Scotch," or "Two straight whiskies, please."

Dialog 4

A : Bartender, B : Guest

A : Would you care for anything to drink, sir?

B : Give Scotch and water.

A : Certainly, sir.
What brand of Scotch would you like, sir?

B : Give me something with a fairly low proof.

A : Yes, sir. Would you like something else?

B : Give me coffee.

A : We are very sorry, sir. We cannot serve coffee here. Would you mind having orange juice or a lemon squash instead?

B : I haven't eaten yet. What would you recommend?

A : Well, let me see. I'd recommend Sherry, Vermouth, Martini, or Manhattan.

B : Please make this one a little sweeter.

Unit 18 Room Service

Dialog 1

A : Room Service, B : Guest

A : Room Service. May I help you, sir?

B : I want to have breakfast tomorrow morning.

A : What would you like to have, sir?

B : Well.... I think I'll have tomato juice, two eggs sunny side-up, buttered toast, and coffee. And a sliced pineapple, please.

A : What time would you like it served, sir?

B : At 7. Is that O.K.?

A : Certainly, sir.

Dialog 2

A : Room Service, B : Guest

A : Good evening, sir. May I help you?

B : Yes, I want dinner in my room.
Let's see, I'll try the T-bone steak.
Do you have vegetable soup?

A : Yes. we do.

B : Okay, bring me vegetable soup, steak, a combination salad and some coffee.

A : Thank you, sir.
May I have your name and room number please.

B : Mr. Baker, room 1825.

Dialog 3

A : Room Service, B : Guest

A : Good morning, room service. May I help you?

B : Hello, we want to have a continental breakfast for two.

A : Very well, sir. Which juice would you like?
Tomato or orange.

B : One orange, please.

A : Alright sir, coffee or tea?

B : Bring us coffee, please.

A : Very well, sir.
May I have your name and room number, please?

B : This is Miller in room 1120.

A : Mr. Miller, 1120.
We'll send your breakfast right away, sir.
Thank you very much.

Airline English

Unit 01 Reservation

1) Request reservation

Dialog A: Airline reservations staff, P: Passenger

A : Good morning, Korean Air.
This is Miss Kim speaking. How may I help you?

P : Hello, I am phoning to find out about flights to New York on May 5th Tuesday.

A : Certainly, sir. I'll check that for you now...... Thank you for waiting, sir. We have seats available in all classes to New York on Tuesday, May 5th. May I have your name, please?

P : Yes, my name is James Dean.

A : Mr. Dean, your name is spelled D-E-A-N, initial D. Is that correct.

P : Yes, That's right.

A : Would you like to travel First, Business or Economy class?

P : Economy Please.

A : Certainly Mr. Dean, I'll reserve that for you now. Thank you for waiting. Mr. Dean May I confirm our return booking at this time.

P : Yes, I plan to return Seoul on June 3th.

A : Thank you. I have confirmed you on Korean Air Flight from New York.

P : That's great. Thank you so much.

A : You are welcome. May I have a telephone number where you can be contacted Mr. Dean?

P : Yes, 02-780-7315.

A : Thank you, sir. You are confirmed Korean Air 007 to New York on May 5 departing Seoul at 2:40 P.M. You will arrive in New York at 2:20 P.M on May 5th. Your return flight is on June 3 on Korean Air flight 008. I have reserved in Economy class for both to and from New York. The fare for this round trip ticket is 1,450,000 Won. You have to reconfirm your reservation at least 72 hours before your departure. Thank you for calling Korean Air.

T : Thank you. Bye-bye.

2) Traveling with children

Dialog A: Airline Reservations staff, P: Passenger

A : United Airlines, may I help you?

P : Oh, good afternoon.
I'd like to reserve seats on a flight to London, Please.

A : How many people will you be traveling ma'am?

P : There are three of us, myself and my two children.

A : May I ask the names and ages of your children?

P : Yes, Jenny is three and David is five month old.

A : So that's Jenny, J-E-N-N-Y and David, D-A-V-I-D. Is that correct?

P : Yes, That's right.

A : Ma'am, if you wish, you may reserve a bassinet for your baby. It is situated in front of your seat. There is no charge for the bassinet or you may reserve a separate seat for David. That would cost 50% of the applicable adult fare. Which would you prefer?

P : Please reserve a separate seat for my baby.

A : Certainly, ma'am. I'll do that for you now. Thank you for waiting. I have reserved three seats for you in non-window section, 23C, D, and E.

P : Yes, good.

A : Would you like me to order any formula or baby food for your baby?

P : No thanks. I'll bring my own food.

A : We also offer children's meals.
Would you like to order one for Jenny?
We have hamburgers and hotdogs.

P : Oh yes, Jenny loves hotdogs.

A : Certainly, ma'am. I'll book that for you now.

P : Thank you.

A : Please do not hesitate to call us if we can be of any further assistance.

P : OK, thank you.

A : You are welcome, ma'am. Thank you for choosing to fly United Airline. I hope you and your children enjoy your flight. Good-bye, ma'am.

P : Good-bye.

3) Transfer flight schedules

Dialog

T: Travel Agency, P: Passenger

T : Good afternoon, How may I help you?

P : Hello, I'm planning a trip to London.
I'd like to get some information, Please.

T : Sure, When do you plan to go to London?

P : I'd like to be there next month.

T : OK. And how long do you want to stay in London?

P : I would like to stay about a week.

T : Fine. Do you want to go any where else?

P : Yes, I'd like to make a few stops in Europe.

T : OK, sure. There's a Euro-trip package that gives you a round trip to London and then three stops in Europe.

P : Can I choose the stops?

T : Certainly. Tell me where you'd like to stop off and we can print out an itinerary for you.

P : Thank you very much for your help.

4) Reconfirmation

Dialog A: Airline agent, P: Passenger

A : Good morning, Northwest airlines, Jennifer speaking. May I help you?

P : Yes.
I'm calling to reconfirm my flight to Los Angles.

A : Certainly, sir, May I have your name and date of travel please?

P : Yes, my name is Jimmy Kim and I will leave Seoul April 10.

A : The spelling is J-I-M-M-Y, Is that correct, Mr. Kim?

P : That's right.

A : Thank you, Mr. Kim. I will check that for you now. Thank you for waiting. You will be flying executive class on our 10 : 30 AM flight to Los angels. We have booked in seat 7 A as you requested. May I confirm that your Seoul contact number is 780-7016?

P : Yes, that is correct.

A : Mr. Kim, thank you for calling Northwest Airlines. I hope you enjoy your flight to Los angels.

P : Thank you, Good-bye.

A : Thank you, Mr. Kim.

5) Canceling reservation

Dialog

A: Airline agent, P: Passenger

A : Smile travel. May I help you?

P : Yes, I'd like to cancel my reservation for the flight form Seoul to New York on Tuesday.

A : May I have your name, please?

P : All right. My name is Andy Kim.

A : Your reservation is cancelled.
Anything else I can do for you?

P : No, thank you.

A : OK, Have a nice day.

Unit • 02 Ticketing

Dialog

A: Airline agent, P: Passenger

A : May I help you?

P : I'd like to purchase my ticket. I already to have a reservation, my reservation number is AZ 203.

A : Your name, Please?

P : Eric Kim.

A : Yes, sir. 3 P.M Tuesday, Northwest Airlines, right?

P : Yes, how much do I pay?

A : It's $1,200 for round-trip.

P : Do you accept Master Card?

A : Sure, may I have credit card, please?

P : Here you are.

A : Would you like to sign, please?

P : Okay.

A : Here is your ticket for Seoul, economy class, on Flight 007 leaving at 3 P.M on May 4th. Anything else I can do for you?

P : No, thanks, anyway.

A : You're welcome. Have a nice day.

Unit • 03 Checking in

Dialog 1

A: Airline agent, P: Passenger

A : Good morning, Sir.
Where are you traveling to this morning?

P : Good morning. I am going to Paris.

A : May I see your passport and ticket, please?

P : Sure, Here you are.

A : Thank you, sir.
Could you put your luggage on the scale, please?

P : OK.

A : Just the two pieces?

P : Yes, just two.

A : That's fine. Would you fill out this name tag and attach it to your bag, please?

P : Sure. Do you have a pen?

A : Here you are.

P : Thanks.

A : Would you like a window seat or on aisle seat.

P : A windows seat, Please.

A : All right, sir. Could you go straight through to the departure lounge now, please? The flight is boarding now.

P : Fine. Thanks a lot.

A : You're welcome. Enjoy your flight.

Dialog 2

A: Airline agent, P: Passenger

A : Good afternoon. How can I help, sir?

P : Good afternoon.
Can I check in here for the flight to London?

A : May I have your ticket and your Passport?

P : Here you are.

A : Thanks.

P : Can I take this briefcase as hand luggage?

A : Yes, as long as it'll go under the seat.

P : Have you got any other luggage?

P : Yes, I've got these two suitcases and this bag.

A : I'm afraid the luggage allowance to London is two-piece. It doesn't involve weight, only the number of pieces.

P : So, how much excess luggage is?

A : Extra charge is $100 for each extra piece that you have.

P : I have one extra luggage, then.

A : Yes, so that will be $100.

P : I see. Do I have to pay now?

A : Yes, please.

P : Here you are.

A : Thank you very much. Where would you like to sit?

A : Window or aisle seat?

P : An aisle seat, please.

A : So that's 17C, that's your boarding pass and your ticket that you'll need to show again at the gate.

P : Thank you.

A : You'll be boarding at Gate 27.
Be sure to be on time, 3 : 30 P.M.

P : Gate 27. Right, Thank you very much.

A : You're welcome.

Unit 04 Security Check-In

Dialog

O: Officer, P: Passenger

O : Please put all carry-on luggages here and step right this way. (Beep) Please empty your pockets and go through. (Beep) Please step this way, ma'am.

P : What was the buzz?

O : The metal detector has sensed a metal object on you. Please step back. What do you have in this pocket?

P : Oh, sorry. I just have some keys.

O : That's fine. Thank you. You can go through.

Unit 05 Pre-boarding Station

Dialog

G: Gate agent, P: Passenger

P : Is this where I check in for Flight 123?

G : Yes, sir. May I see your boarding pass, please?

P : Yes, here it is.

G : Your seat is 37C, economy class. Boarding will start in a few minutes. Here is your boarding pass.

P : Thank you.

G : You're welcome.

Unit 06 Check-In Announcements

1) Government formalities for departure

May I have your attention, please? Passengers who have not finished the formalities for departure are requested to come to the customs office immediately. Your forms must be completed and checked before you board the plane. We have airline employees available to assist you. Promptly complete this necessary part of your flight. Thank you.

2) Check-in

May I have your attention, please?

Passengers for ______ Airlines Flight ______ bound for ______, please go through check-in and baggage check at check-in counter. Thank you.

3) Security check-in

May I have your attention, please? Passengers for ______ Airlines Flight bound for, please have your travel card and passport ready and proceed to departure lounge. Thank you.

4) Final call security check-in

May I have your attention please? This is the final call for ______ Airlines Flight ______ bound for ______. All remaining passengers who finished check-in at the counter, please get on board immediately through the security check in the lounge. Thank you.

5) Departure delayed

(1) With new departure time

May I have your attention, please? We are sorry to announce that ______ Airlines Flight ______ bound for ______ will be delayed due to dense fog(heavy snow, heavy rain, strong winds). The new departure time will be ______. Thank you.

(2) Without new arrival time

May I have your attention, please? We are sorry to announce that ______ Airlines, Flight ______ bound for ______ will be delayed due to dense fog (heavy snow, heavy rain, strong winds). Further information will be announced as soon as possible. Thank you.

6) Departure cancelled

May I have your attention, please? We are sorry to announce that ______ Airlines, Flight ______ bound for ______ has been cancelled due to dense fog (heavy snow, heavy rain, strong winds). Passengers who want to make a reservation for another flight please come to the information counter. Thank you.

7) Boarding

Your attention, please. ______ Airlines announces the departure of Flight ______ bound for. Those with first-class tickets, small children or needing assistance please board at this time. Our staff is ready to assist you. We will call for other passengers in a few minutes. Thank you for flying ______ Airlines today.

Unit • 07 Passenger Boarding

1) At the door

Dialog

C : Cabin crew, P: Passenger

C : Good morning, sir. Welcome aboard.

P : Good morning. Where is 53H?

C : Please take the other aisle.

Your seat is in the back of the cabin.

P : Thanks.

C : You're welcome, sir.

2) In the cabin

Dialog 1

C: Cabin crew, P: Passenger

C : Good afternoon, ma'am.

May I see your boarding pass, please?

P : Here you are.

C : Your seat number is 16 A. This way, please.

May I help you with tour bag?

P : Here you are. Thank you(Passenger blocking the aisle / Standing in the aisle).

C : Excuse me, ma'am. May I help you?

P : No, I'm just stretching.

C : Would you please step aisle to let these people through?

P : OK, I'll sit.

C : Thank you, ma'am.

Dialog 2

C: Cabin crew P: Passenger

C : May I help you with your belongings, ma'am?

P : Yes, please. Thank you.

C : My pleasure. May I see your boarding pass, please?

P : Here you are.

C : Thank you. This way, please. Here you are. There is your seat. Would you mind keeping your bags under your seats, please? That's a beautiful girl. She is so cute.

P : Thank you so much.

C : You're welcome. If you need anything during the flight, please let us know.

Dialog 3

C: Cabin crew, P: Passenger

C : Would you like a baby bassinet?

P : Yes, Please.

C : Certainly, ma'am. I will get one for you right after take-off for your baby's safety.... Here is your bassinet. We also have diapers, bottles, baby food and formula. If you need anything, please let us know. Have a nice flight.

Dialog 4

C: Cabin crew, P: Passenger

P : Excuse me, can I have a glass of water?

C : Certainly, Sir. I'll get it for you right away. I'm sorry to have kept you waiting. Here is your drink, sir.

(ordering a drink before take-off)

C : What can I do for you?

P : I would like to order a drink.

C : Sir, We cannot serve drink before take-off.

P : Oh, I would really like one now.

C : I will serve you a drink as soon as possible after take-off.

P : O.K.

C : Don't worry, take-off is in a few minutes.

P : Great.

Dialog 5

C: Cabin crew, P: Passenger

P : Can I use lavatory now?

C : I'm sorry, sir. But would you mind using the lavatory after take-off?

P : I can't stand it.

C : All right, but please hurry. We'll be taking off soon.

Unit • 08 Seating Guide

1) Separated passenger

Dialog 1

C: Cabin crew, P: Passenger

P : Excuse me, my friend and I were assigned separate seats. Do you have any empty seats together?

C : I see, sir. We have some empty seats in the middle of the cabin. Would that be all right, sir?

P : That's fine, thank you.

C : This way, please. Here you are.
Have a nice flight, sir.

Dialog 2

C: Cabin crew, P: Passenge

P : My wife sitting over there, and we want to sit together.

C : I'II see if that can be arranged after take-off, sir. Thank you for waiting. Here are empty seats in the back of the cabin. It is a smoking zone. Would that be all right, sir?

P : Yes, that will be fine, thank you.

C : You're welcome. This way, please.
Here are your seats. Have a nice flight, sir.

Dialog 3

C: Cabin crew, P: Passenger

P1 : My girl friend is sitting over there, and we want to sit together. Is that possible?

C : I'll see if it can be arranged, sir.
Where is your girl friend sitting?

P1 : Just across the aisle there.

C : Just a moment, please.
Excuse me, sir. I am sorry to bother you. But we have a couple who been assigned separate seats. Would you mind changing seats so they can sit

together?

P2 : No, I don't. Where should I sit?

C : Thank you very much, sir. This way, please.
I'm sorry for the inconvenience, sir.
Would you care for something to drink?

P2 : No, thank you.

C : Sir, this gentleman is willing to change seats with you. This way, please. Here you are, sir.

P1 : Thank you. I appreciate it.

C : My pleasure, sir. Have a nice flight.

2) Changing seats

Dialog 1

C: Cabin crew, P: Passenger

P : May I change my seat?

C : Yes, you may.
We have lots of empty seats at the back.

P : I'd like a window seat.

C : Please come this way, sir.

Dialog 2

C: Ccabin crew, P: Passenger

P : Do you have empty seats in front of the cabin?

C : Just a moment please. I'll see what's available. We have empty seats in the middle of the cabin in the non-smoking zone. Would that be all right, sir?

P : Yes, that will be fine.

C : This way, please.

3) Wrong seats

Dialog C: Cabin crew, P: Passenger

P1 : Excuse me, I think this is my seat.

C : (To P1) Excuse me, ma'am. May I see your boarding pass, please? I'm sorry, but you are the wrong seat. Your seat is behind this one.
Would you mind changing seats, please?

P2 : Sure, Where is my seat?

C : (To P1) It is yours, ma'am. Have a pleasant flight. (To P2) This way, please. Your seat is right here, sir. I'm sorry for the inconvenience. Have a nice flight, sir.

4) Double seating

Dialog

C: Cabin crew, P: Passenger

P1 : Excuse me, this passenger is in my seat.

C : May I see your boarding pass, please? Thank you. I'm sorry, but I'm afraid there has been a mistake in seating arrangement.
(To P2) This way, please.
Would you mind waiting here, sir? I'll check it for you immediately.... Thank you for waiting. Your seat is arranged, sir. It's 42H. This way, please. I'm sorry for the inconvenience, sir. Would you care for something to drink, sir?

5) Luggage in the aisle

Dialog 1

C: Cabin crew, P: Passenger

C : Excuse me, sir. Is this bag yours?

P : Yes, it is.

C : I'm sorry, sir, but we have to keep the aisle open (or clear).
Would you mind keeping your bag under your seat, please?

P : Sure.

C : Thank you. Have a nice flight.

Dialog 2

C: Cabin crew, P: Passenger

P : Excuse me. Where can I put my bag? It doesn't fit under my seat and the overhead compartment is full.

C : Would you like me to keep your bag in the back of the cabin?

P : Yes, would you do that? Thank you.

C : My pleasure. Have a pleasure flight.

Dialog 3

C: Cabin crew P: Passenger

C : Excuse me.

P : Yes?

C : I'm afraid you can't leave your bag there.

P : Why not? It's not in anyone's way.

C : No, but it might be.
You're sitting next to the emergency exit.

P : So where do I put it?
I'll need things in it during the flight.

C : I think you'll find there's enough room to put it

under your seat.

6) Luggage in the seat

Dialog C: Cabin crew, P: Passenger

C : Excuse me, ma'am. We'll be taking off shortly. It may fall out. Would you mind keeping your bag under your seat, please?

P : Sure.

C : Thank you.

7) Luggage in the overhead compartment

Dialog 1 C: Cabin crew, P: Passenger

P : (putting a heavy bag in the overhead compartment)

C : Excuse me, sir. Would you mind keeping your bag under your seat, please? It might fall out during the flight.

Oh, that's all right.

Thank you, sir. Have a nice flight.

Dialog 2 C: Cabin crew, P: Passenger

C : Can I help you?

P : I can't get my rucksack into the overhead compartment.

C : Don't worry. I'll do it for you.

Unit • 09 Preparations for Take-off

1) Seat belt check

Dialog 1 C: Cabin crew, P: Passenger

P : (seat belt not fastened)

C : Excuse me, ma'am. Would you please fasten your seatbelt? We'll be taking off shortly (...). Thank you. Have a nice flight.

Dialog 2 C: Cabin crew, P: Passenger

C : Excuse me, ma'am Would you mind holding your baby outside your seatbelt?

P : OK.

C : Thank you.

2) Tray table / Seat back

Dialog

C: Cabin crew, P: Passenger

C : Excuse me, sir. Would you please close your tray table for the take off, please?

P : OK.

C : Thank you.

C : Excuse me, sir. Would you mind returning your seat back to the upright position, please?

P : Is that all right?

C : Sure.

3) Newspaper service

Dialog 1

C: Cabin crew, P: Passenger

C : Would you like a newspaper or a magazine, sir?

P : Yes, do you have the times?

C : Yes, here you are.

P : Thank you.

C : You're welcome.

Dialog 2

C: Cabin crew, P: Passenger

P : Can I have the Financial Times?

C : I'm sorry, but I'm afraid we have run out of the Financial Times. Would you care for the Times instead?

P : Oh, that's fine.

C : Here is your newspaper. Have a nice flight, sir.

4) Delay in departure

Dialog

C: Cabin crew, P: Passenger

P : What's the reason for the delay?

C : I'm sorry, sir. We are waiting for a few more passengers to board the aircraft. We'll be taking off as soon as they arrive.

Unit 10 Before Take-off Announcement

1) Boarding

Good Morning (afternoon, evening) ladies and gentlemen.

This is _____ Airlines _____ bound for _____. All heavy or fragile items must be places under your seat, and be careful when you open the overhead bin to prevent items inside falling out. Thank you for your cooperation.

2) Takeoff delayed

(1) Ladies and gentlemen. Because of the current weather conditions at _____ airport (nation), our departure is going to be delayed about _____ minutes. We'll take off as soon as possible. Thank you.

(2) Ladies and gentlemen. The weather condition at airport have not improved yet. The decision will be made following the _____ o'clock weather check. Thank you for your understanding and patience.

3) Welcome

(1) Ladies and gentlemen, welcome abroad _____ Airlines flight _____ bound for _____. Today's flight time be about _____ hour(s) _____ minute(s) following take-off. The captain of this flight is _____

and this is your flight attendant _____. Now, please make sure that your seatback is in the upright position, your tray table is closed and your seatbelt is fastened. And we recommend that you continue to fasten your seatbelt while seated during the flight. Also, refrain from using any electronic devices during take-off and landing for safety reasons. Your cooperation will be much appreciated. If there is anything we can do for you, please let us know. We wish you a pleasant flight. Thank you.

(2) Good morning, ladies and gentlemen. Welcome aboard Airlines Flight _____ bound for _____. Commanding your plane this morning is Captain _____. I'm Chief Purser _____. Please fasten your seat belt, return your seat to the upright position. And observe the no-smoking sign until it is turned off. Also refrain from using any electronic devices during take-off and landing for safety reason. We are waiting for clearance from the air traffic control tower. We expert to take off in a few minutes. If there is anything we can do for you, please let us know.

4) Safety demonstration

(1) Video : Ladies and gentlemen, We would like to familiarize you with the safety features of this aircraft. Please pay attention to the following video. Thank you.

(2) Demonstration : Ladies and gentlemen, We would like to inform you of the safety features of this aircraft. In the case of emergency evacuation, there are emergency exits on both sides of the aircraft. In an emergency situation, emergency lights located in the ceiling and aisles will be turned on automatically to guide you to the exits. Please take a moment to identify the nearest exit from your seat.

To fasten your seat belt, please insert the metal tongue into the buckle and tighten the belt by pulling the loose end. To release your seat belt, lift up the metal cover.

If cabin pressure is interrupted for any reason, an overhead panel will be opened automatically, exposing several oxygen masks When your mask appears, pull the mask toward you and cover nose and mouth with the mask. Then adjust the headband to fit your head.

In preparation for ditching, a life vest is located under your seat. To put the vest on, slip it over your head. Take the strap and put it around your waist, then fasten. Tighten your vest by pulling the strap. Your life vest can be inflated by pulling down on the two red knobs or by blowing into the inflation tubes on either side. But, please do not inflate the vest while inside the aircraft.

Now please take a moment to review the safety features by looking through the safety instruction card located in your seat pocket. Thank you.

5) Takeoff

Ladies and gentlemen, we will be taking off shortly. Please make sure that your seat belt is fastened. Thank you.

6) Restriction on using electronic service

Ladies and gentlemen, you may now use your electronic devices, but please refrain from using portable phone, television, pagers, wireless electronic games and toys, and other type of radio or communication devices during the flight. For further information, please contact your flight attendant. Thank you.

Unit 11 Earphone and Travel Service

1) Hot towel service

Dialog 1 C: Cabin crew, P: Passenger

C : Please be careful. It's very hot, sir.

P : Thank you.

Dialog 2 C: Cabin crew, P: Passenger

C : Excuse me, sir. Have you finished with your towel?

P : Yes, thank you.

C : (taking towel) You're welcome, sir.

Dialog 3 C: Cabin crew, SP: Sleeping Passenger

C : Excuse me, sir. Would you care for a hot towel? We'll be serving dinner soon.

SP : Oh, thank you.

2) Earphone service

Dialog 1 C: Cabin crew, P: Passenger

C : Excuse me sir. Here your earphone set.

P : No, thank you.

C : Are you sure? It's free of charge.

Dialog 2 C: Cabin crew, P: Passenger

C : Would you care for an earphone set, ma'am?

P : Do you charge for it?

C : No, ma'am. It's free of charge.

P : Alright, I'll have one. Thank you.

C : You're welcome, ma'am.

Unit 12 Meal and Beverage Service

1) Beverage service

Dialog 1 C: Cabin crew, P: Passenger

C : Would you like something to drink?

P : What kind of juice do you have?

C : We have tomato, pineapple and orange juice.

P : Orange juice, please.

C : Here is your orange juice. Enjoy your drink.

P : Thank you.

C : You're welcome.

Dialog 2

C: Cabin crew, P: Passenger

C : Good morning, ma'am.
Would care for something to drink?

P : Yes, I'd like to have diet coke, please.

C : How about a diet Pepsi?

P : That's Ok.

C : Here you go.

P : Thank you.

Dialog 3

C: Cabin crew, P: Passenger

P : Excuse me, I am afraid my drink is too strong (weak).

C : I'm sorry, sir. I'll add some more tonics. (Whisky, Rum, Gin, Vodka, etc) How is it now, sir?

P : Good.

C : I'm sorry for the inconvenience, sir.

Dialog 4

C: Cabin crew, P: Passenger

C : Would you care for something to drink?

P : Can I have some champagne?

C : I'm sorry, ma'am. Champagne is not service on the flight. Would you like to drink something else?

P : Oh, I see. I'll have beer, then.

2) Meal service

Dialog 1

C: Cabin crew, P: Passenger

C : Excuse me, ma'am. We have a choice of beef and chicken for dinner. Which one would you prefer?

P : I'd like beef.

C : Here you are, ma'am. Enjoy your meal.
(When beef entrée run out.)

P : I'll have beef, please.

C : I am sorry. We are all out of beef just now, but we have chicken. Would that be all right?

Dialog 2

C: Cabin crew, P: Passenger

P : Excuse me. This steak isn't cooked well.

C : I am sorry. Let me have your meal back.
I'll take care of it for you.

P : Please.

C : I will get your meal as soon as possible.

Dialog 3

C: Cabin crew, P1, P2: Passenger

P1 : Miss, I requested a vegetarian meal.

C : I see, sir. I'll check on your meal right away....
Thank you for waiting, Mr. Brown. Here you are.
Enjoy your meal, sir.

C : Excuse me, sir. Did you request a kosher meal?

P2 : Yes, I did.

C : Here is your meal. May I unwrap your meal box
and heat it up for you?

P2 : Yes, Please.

Dialog 4

C: Cabin crew, P: Passenger

C : We have a choice of a Korean dish or a Western dish. Which would you prefer?

P : What is the Korean dish?

C : It is called Bi-Bim-Bap. It is rice, vegetables, sesame oil, and hot pepper paste mixed together. If you don't like spicy food, you can eat it without the hot pepper paste

P : Okay, I'll try that.

C : Here you are. Enjoy your meal.

3) Wine service

Dialog

C: Cabin crew, P: Passenger

C : Would you care for some wine, sir?

P : Yes, Please.

C : We have red and white wine.
Which would you like?

P : Red, please.

C : Here you are. Enjoy your wine....
Would you like some more wine?

4) Coffee and Tea service

Dialog C: Cabin crew, P: Passenger

C : Would you care for a cup of coffee?

P : Yes, please.

C : May I have your cup, please? Here you are.

P : Thank you.

C : Would you care for a cup of tea?

P : Yes, please.

C : Here you are.
Would you like some lemon with your tea?

P : Yes, please. And my wife wants coffee.

C : Another cabin attendant will be here with coffee, sir.
Just a moment, please.

5) Meal tray pick-up

Dialog C: Cabin crew P: Passenger

C : Excuse me, sir. Are you finished with your meal?

P : Yes, I am.

C : May I take your meal?

P : Please.

C : Did you enjoy your meal, sir?

P : Yes, I enjoyed it very much.

C : Are you finished with your meal?

P : No, I'm not finished yet.

C : I'm sorry sir. Please take your time and enjoy your meal. Would you like some more coffee?

P : Yes, Please.

C : I'll get some for you right away.
Just a moment please. Here you are.

Unit 13 In-Flight Music and Movie

Dialog 1

C: Cabin crew, P: Passenger

P : When are you showing the movie today?

C : The movie will be shown after the meal, sir.

P : What kind of movie do you have?

C : This pamphlet will show you today's in-flight movie program, sir.

P : Oh, I see. But I can't see the movie screen from this seat. Are there any empty seats in the front of the cabin?

C : I'm sorry, but I'm afraid all the seats are occupied. I'm sorry for the inconvenience, sir.

P : Will you ask if someone is willing to exchange seats?

C : Yes, I'll let you know in a few minutes.

Dialog 2

C: Cabin crew, P: Passenger

C : Excuse me, are you planning on watching the movie?

P : No, I plan to sleep.

C : In that case, would you mind changing seats with a gentleman who wants to watch the movie?

P : I want an aisle seat.

C : He has an aisle seat farther back in the cabin.

P : Okay, then I suppose I will move.

C : Thank you, after the movie you may return to this seat if you would like.

P : That would be fine.

Dialog 3

C: Cabin crew, P: Passenger

P : Excuse me, but I don't think my earphone is working.

C : I'll check the volume control and channel selector. Can you hear it now, sir?

P : No, still nothing at all.

C : Just a moment. I'll get a new set of earphones for you. Would you also like to move to this seat over here? The sound system might work better here.

P : Yes, I can hear it now.

C : How did you get it work?

P : I simply plugged it in.

Dialog 4

C: Cabin crew, P: Passenger

C : Excuse me, sir, are you going to watch the movie?

P : Yes, I think I will.

C : Then would you like to change your seat? I'm afraid you won't be able to see the screen very well from this seat, sir. A seat in the middle of the cabin is unoccupied.

P : Yes, I guess I had better.

C : Please follow me.

P : Thank you.

Dialog 5

C: Cabin crew, P: Passenger

C : What can I do for you, sir?

P : I would like to watch the movie, but I can't find the channel.

C : Let me help you.

P : I can hear the movie, but it is in Japanese.
I would like to hear it in English.

C : Of course, that would be another channel.

P : Yes, that is good.

C : Okay, anything else?

Unit 14 Service and Comfort

Dialog 1

C: Cabin crew, P: Passenger

P : Is there any other seat I could take to make it easier for my baby?

C : Of course, do you need an extra blanket?

Dialog 2

C: Cabin crew, P: Passenger

P : How do I return my seat to the upright position?

C : Please push this button and lean forward, sir.
Would you like a blanket, sir?

P : Yes, please.

C : How about some coffee or tea?

P : Coffee, please.

C : Would you care for a newspaper or magazine?

P : Do you have Cho-Sun-Il-Bo?

C : Certainly, sir. Just a moment, please.

Dialog 3

C: Cabin crew, P: Passenger

C : Do you need something, sir?

P : Yes, do you have any playing cards?

C : As a matter of fact, we do have some.

P : Could we have two decks, please?

C : I'll bring them right away.

P : Thanks.

C : Here they are, sir. Have fun.

P : This will help the time go quickly.

Dialog 4

C: Cabin crew, P: Passenger

C : Good morning. Are you enjoying the flight?

P : Yes, it's been great.

C : Is this your first visit to Korea?

P : No, I visited Korea during the Olympics in 1988. I enjoyed it very much.

C : I see. I hope you enjoy your stay in Korea again.

Unit 15 Sick Passenger Handling

Dialog 1

C: Cabin crew, P: Passenger

P : Excuse me. I get airsick very easily, and I feel a bit nauseous right now. Is there anything for that?

C : I'm sorry to hear that, sir.
We have Bonaling-A. Would that be all right?

P : Yes, that's all right.

C : Are you allergic to any kind of medicine?

P : No, I'm not.

C : Just a moment please. (...)

C : How many tablets would you like?

P : I'll have two, please.

C : Here you are. I hope you feel better soon.

Dialog 2

C: Cabin crew, P: Passenger

P : Excuse me.
Do you have anything for indigestion?

C : Yes, sir. We have Zestan on board. Are you allergic to any type of medicine?

P : No, I am not. May I have some please?

C : Certainly, sir. I'll get it for you right away. (...)
Here you are. I hope you get well soon.

Dialog 3

C: Cabin crew, P: Passenger

C : Did you push the button for an attendant?

P : Yes, I have a terrible headache.

C : May I bring you some aspirin?

P : Please do.

C : I'll be back in a moment.

P : Aspirin, wonderful!

C : Let me turn this light out of your eyes.

P : Thank you, you have been so helpful.

Unit 16 In-Flight Sales

Dialog 1

C: Cabin crew, P: Passenger

C : Would you like to buy any duty-free items?

P : What kind of duty-free items do you have?

C : Here is a shopping guide, sir. (...)
Would you like to buy anything, sir?

P : Yes, what do you have?

C : This shopping guide will show you the selections we have.

Dialog 2

C: Cabin crew, P: Passenger

P : What kind of cigarettes do you have?

C : We have Marlboro, Mild Seven, and so on, sir.
Here is a shopping guide, sir.

P : How much are they?

C : Most cigarettes are twelve to fifteen dollars a carton.
(...)

(Items not available)

P : I'd like to buy two bottles of Johnnie Walker Black.

C : I'm sorry, sir. They are all sold out.
Would you like Chivas Regal, instead?

P : Yes, that will be all right.

C : It will be twenty-five dollars, sir.

Dialog 3

C: Cabin crew, P: Passenger

P : Do you know how much perfume I can take into Hong Kong?

C : This pamphlet will show the perfume allowance for Hong Kong, sir. You may take in 60ml of perfume.

P : Oh, I see. Thank you.

C : You're welcome, sir.

Dialog 4

C: Cabin crew, P: Passenger

C : May I take your order for any duty-free items, sir?

P : Yes, what do you have?

C : We have alcohol, souvenirs, cosmetics, cigarettes and perfume for sale, sir. This shopping guide will tell about our in-flight sales, sir.

Dialog 5

C: Cabin crew, P: Passenger

P : I'm sorry, but all I have is a 100-dollar bill. Do you have change?

C : Oh, I'm sorry. I'm afraid I don't have change right now, sir. I will bring your change as soon as possible. Would that be all right? (Write down seat number, the amount received, cost of item and name.) I am sorry to have kept you waiting, sir. Here is your change, $60. Is that sir?

P : Thank you.

C : You're welcome, sir.

Dialog 6

C: Cabin crew, P: Passenger

P : Excuse me, would I be able to get a refund on these cosmetics?

C : Could you tell me where you bought them, sir?

P : I bought them at the airport duty-free shop.

C : I'm sorry, but I'm afraid we can only give refunds on items purchased on our flight, sir.

P : I see. Thank you.

Unit 17 CIQ Information

Dialog 1

C: Cabin crew, P: Passenger

P : Excuse me. When I left Korea, they put this landing card in my passport.

C : Are you a resident?

P : Yes, I am.

C : Please just fill in our flight number, and the place of departure.

Dialog 2

C: Cabin crew, P: Passenger

P : Excuse me, I'll be staying in England for one week. Do I need to fill out this card?

C : Yes, sir. All passengers entering England must fill out the landing card. Would you like me to help you with it, sir?

P : Yes, please, that would be very helpful thank you.

Dialog 3

C: Cabin crew, P: Passenger

P : I'll be at Narita airport only for two hours and then

I'll be flying on to Honolulu. Do I need this card?

C : No, you don't have to fill out the card.

Unit 18 Destination City Information

Dialog 1

C: Cabin crew, P: Passenger

P : Is there any time difference between Seoul and Taipei?

C : Seoul is one hour ahead of Taipei.

P : How about between Seoul and Tokyo?

C : There's no time difference between them.

Dialog 2

C: Cabin crew, P: Passenger

P : What's the arrival time in Seoul?

C : 6:30 in the morning.

P : How long does it take to get to downtown Seoul from the airport?

C : It takes about one hour by taxi, but it depends on the traffic. There are two kinds of taxis, regular and deluxe.

P : Is there any bus service available?

C : Certainly, ma'am. There is an airport but which comes every 20 minutes. It takes about one hour to downtown.

P : Thank you.

C : You're welcome. Have a nice stay in Korea.

Dialog 3

C: Cabin crew, P: Passenger

P : Do you know any good places for shopping in Seoul?

C : I would recommend Itaewon. You can get many souvenirs, inexpensive clothes, and shoes. People there can speak English.

P : I see. What else would you recommend for me?

C : Namdaemun Market is another place you can enjoy shopping. You can get everything. The items are cheap, but please make sure to bargain.

Unit 19 Landing and Deplaning

Dialog 1

C: Cabin crew, P: Passenger

C : Excuse me, sir. Would you please return to your seat? We will be landing shortly.

P : Could I use the lavatory now?

C : Yes, go ahead, sir.

P : Thanks.

C : Remember to fasten your seatbelt when you return to your seat.

Dialog 2

C: Cabin crew, P: Passenger

C : May I have your earphone set, please?

P : Yes, of course.

C : Sir, would you mind returning your seat to the upright position for landing, please? Thank you. Did you enjoy our flight?

P : Yes, it was great.

C : We hope you will fly with us again soon.

P : I hope so, too.

Dialog 3

C: Cabin crew, P: Passenger

C : Excuse me. Have you finished your drink?

P : Yes, I have.

C : Would you mind keeping your bag under your seat?
We must keep the aisle open, sir.
We are in preparation for landing now.

P : Yes, I'll be happy to put my bag under the seat.

C : We appreciate it.

Dialog 4

C: Cabin crew, P: Passenger

C : The Captain requests that everyone remain seated until the plane comes to a complete stop.

P : I'm worried about my connecting flight.

C : When is your next flight?

P : It is departing in 20 minutes.

C : Do you know which gate?

P : It is in my ticket information.

Unit 20 En-Route Announcements

1) Service plan

Ladies and gentlemen, we'd like to inform you of our in-flight services on today's flight to _____. In a few minutes, we will be serving cocktails and soft drinks followed by breakfast (lunch/dinner/a snack). After the meal service, duty free sales will be followed, and a (two) movie(s) for your entertainment. _____ hours before arrival, breakfast (lunch/dinner/a snack) will be served. For details of the service procedures, please refer to the in-flight magazine in your seat pocket. We wish you a pleasant flight. Thank you.

2) Meal and beverage

Ladies and gentlemen, now we are flying (over 10,000 ft.) to the cruising altitude. Our flight attendants will be serving you cold drinks (breakfast/lunch/dinner). We wish you a pleasant flight. Thank you.

3) In-Flight movie

Ladies and gentlemen, we will be showing you a movie in a short moment. The movie for today is ____. Thank you, and enjoy.

4) Turbulence

Ladies and gentlemen, this is your captain speaking. We are now having (expecting) some turbulence (in a few minutes). So please return to your seats and fasten your seat belts. We will be out of this turbulence in about ____ minutes. Thank you for your cooperation.

5) In-Flight duty-free sales

Ladies and gentlemen, in a few minutes we will begin our duty-free sales. If you would like to purchase any items, please let us know as the duty-free sales cart passes by your seat. For further information, please feel free to contact your flight attendants. Thank you.

6) Flying over scenic spots

Ladies and gentlemen, this is your captain speaking. In a few minutes you will be able to see ______ on the right (left) side of the aircraft. Thank you.

7) Document

Ladies and gentlemen, for entering ____, please have your passport and other entry documents ready.

(1) Entering Korea : All nationalities are required to fill out both a customs form and an arrival card before entering Korea. Passengers who have baggage arriving on another aircraft or by ship must fill out two customs form. After claiming your baggage at Incheon International Airport, passengers must preceed through either the green or red customs inspection lines. Passengers not carrying items valued at more than 400 US dollars, firearms, explosives, narcotics, North Korean propaganda or articles subject to quarantine can clear customs through the green lines. If you have more than 10,000 US dollars or the equivalent in foreign currency, you must report that amount on the customs form and pass through the red lines. For further information, please contact your flight attendant. Thank you.

(2) Entering the Unites States : Ladies and gentlemen, for entering the United States, you will need to have your passport and other entry documents ready. The United States government requires that all passengers except for US citizens, Canadian citizens, US green card holders, and passengers with US immigrant visas complete an arrival card. All nationalities must fill out the US customs form before entering the Unites States. Families traveling together only need to fill out one form each for their entire family. Also, passengers having more than 10,000 US dollars or the equivalent in foreign currency or traveler's checks must declare that amount on the form. Those passengers with connecting flight are also required to pick up all checked baggage and clear customs here in _____ before your next flight. If there are any questions, please let us know. Thank you.

8) Headphone collection

Ladies and gentlemen, we are now approaching our final destination into ____ airport. We ask you to return your seat back to the upright position, close your tray table, and fasten your seatbelt.

This includes our audio entertainment program. We hope your have enjoyed the in-flight music programs.

Your flight attendants will now pick up the headphones shortly. We appreciate your cooperation. Thank you.

9) Destination approaching

(1) **Destination approaching** : Ladies and gentlemen, we are approaching our destination into _____ airport. Please return to your seat and fasten your seat belt. Also, please turn off all electronic devices at this point.

(2) (2.1) **Transit passengers** : For those passengers continuing on to ___, please remain seated on board. We should be on the ground for about ____ minutes.

(2.2) For those passengers continuing on to ___, please exit and take a transit card. Also please take all of your belongings with you. Bags and valuables cannot be left on board. We should be on the ground for about ____ minutes. We'll make an announcement in the transit area when we are ready to re-board.

Unit 21 Landing

(1) Ladies and gentlemen. We are now making our final approach. Please make sure that your seat is in the up right position, your tray table is close, and your seatbelt is fastened. Thank you for your cooperation.

(2) We are now approaching Incheon International Airport. We wish to remind you that taking pictures over the airport is strictly prohibited according to the order of the Korean Government Defense Authorities. Please fasten your seatbelt and remain in your seat until the plane comes to a complete stop.

Unit 22 Farewell

Ladies and gentlemen, we have just landed at ______ airport. The local time in _____ is _____ p.m. (a.m.). For your safety, please remain seated with your seatbelt fastened, until we come to a complete stop and the captain turns off the seatbelt sign. Please be sure to take all of your belongings with you when you exit. And be careful when opening the overhead bins, since bags may fall down. I would like to express our sincere thanks to all of you for flying ______ airlines. We look forward to serving you again in the near future. We wish you a pleasant stay in ______. Good-bye.

Unit · 23 Deplaning

Thank you for waiting, ladies and gentlemen. You may now exit through the forward door and please make sure to take all of your belongings with you when you exit. We wish you a pleasant day (evening) and thank you once again for flying ___ airlines.

Unit · 24 Immigration

Dialog 1

O: Officer, P: Passenger

O : Do you live in Korea?

P : Yes, I do.

O : What was the purpose of your visit to England?

P : It was a business trip.

O : Was this your first visit?

P : No, I've been here twice before.

O : OK, thank you.

Dialog 2

O: Officer, P: Passenger

O : Good morning, sir.
May I see your passport and landing card, please?

P : Sure, here it is.

O : What's the purpose of your trip, sir?

P : Business.

O : How long do your intend to stay?

P : About three weeks at most.

O : OK, sir. You may go to customs now.

P : Thank you very much.

Dialog 3

O: Officer, P: Passenger

O : Please give me your landing card and let me see your passport.

P : Here they are.

O : Thank you. What is your nationality?

P : Korean.

O : How long will you stay here?

P : A couple of months.
Is the customs examination held here?

O : Yes, do you have anything to declare?

P : Only my personal baggage.

Unit 25 Baggage Claim

Dialog 1

O: Officer, P: Passenger

P : Excuse me. My luggage hasn't arrived.

O : What is your flight number?

P : I was in flight 180, British Airways.

O : Can you describe it?

P : Sure. It is gray and there is a blue ribbon on it.
My name is also on the side of it.

O : Do you have a baggage claiming tag?

P : Yes, here you are.

O : Well, we'll let you know as soon as we find it.

P : Please do.

Dialog 2

O: Officer, P: Passenger

O : May I help you?

P : Yes, only one of my bags is here.

O : How many bags did you have?

P : I had two bags.

O : Please fill out this form.

P : OK.

O : We will notify you when we find your bag.

P : OK. I really need it.

Dialog 3

O: Officer, P: Passenger

P : Excuse me, I need assistance.

O : How may I help you?

P : My bag is damaged.

O : Oh, I am sorry. Please complete this form.

P : OK. Will the process take long?

O : No.

P : I am only in Dublin for two days.

O : I'm sorry for the inconvenience, sir.

Dialog 4

O: Officer, P: Passenger

O : May I help you?

P : I hope so.

O : What can I do?

P : I picked up the wrong bag by mistake.
It looked just like mine.

O : What is the name on the tag?

P : Mr. Charles Park

O : I'll page Mr. Park right away, and have him report here.

P : That would be great, perhaps he has my bag.

Unit 26 Customs

Dialog 1

O: Officer, P: Passenger

O : Do you have anything to declare?

P : Yes, I have something to declare. I have a bottle of Korean drink. It's for my friend.

O : What is its approximate value?

P : About 15 pounds.

O : Open your bag, please. They are pills, aren't they?

P : Yes, they are for high blood pressure.

O : May I see the label?

P : Yes, of course.

Dialog 2

O: Officer, P: Passenger

P : Excuse me.

O : Yes.

P : Can you tell me where I should go to get out? I have nothing to declare.

O : Then, go through the green channel.

P : I see. Thank you.

O : You're welcome.

P : This way?

O : Yes, straight ahead.

Dialog 3

O: Officer, P: Passenger

P : What are the articles liable to duty?

O : They are tobacco, liquors, jewels, watches, cameras and so forth. Do you have any?

P : No, I haven't.

How many cigarettes am I allowed to take with me?

O : The limit is one hundred.

P : I have well under that limit.

O : Please proceed.

Unit 27 Money Exchange Counter

Dialog 1

O: Officer, P: Passenger

P : I'd like to change Korean won into pounds sterling, please.

O : Sure, how much?

P : Fifty thousand won. What's the exchange rate?

O : One pound is about 1,800 won.
Please fill out this form.

P : May I use your pen?

Dialog 2

O: Officer, P: Passenger

O : May I help you, sir?

P : Please exchange this traveler's check for cash.

O : May I see your passport, please?

P : Yes, and here is the check.

O : Please sign your name here. Here's your money.

P : Thank you.

Dialog 3

O: Officer, P: Passenger

P : I would like to exchange 500 pounds.

O : How would you like it?

P : I would like six fifty-pound notes and ten twenty-pound notes please.

O : Here you are.

P : Thank you.

Dialog 4

O: Officer, P: Passenger

P : Could I break ten pounds into some small coins?

O : How would you like it?

P : Can I have one five and five one-pound coins please?

O : Here you go, one five and five one-pound coins.

P : Thank you very much.

O : You're welcome.

Unit·28 Check-Out Announcements

1) Arrival

May I have your attention please? ____ Airlines Flight _____ is now arriving from ____. Thank you.

2) Paging

May I have your attention, please? Mr. ___, Mr. ___ incoming passenger from ___, please come to the ___ Airlines information counter.

3) Arrival delayed

(1) With new arrival time

Ladies and gentlemen, may I have your attention, please? We are sorry to announce that ____ Airlines Flight ____ from ____ will be delayed due to dense fog (heavy snow, heavy rain, strong winds). The new arrival time will be _____. Thank you.

(2) Without new arrival time

Ladies and gentlemen, may I have your attention, please? We are sorry to announce that Airlines Flight _____ from _____ will be delayed due to dense fog (heavy snow, heavy rain, strong winds). Further information will be announced as soon as possible. Thank you.

4) Arrival cancelled

May I have your attention please? We are sorry to announce that ______ Airlines Flight _____ from _____ has been cancelled due to dense fog (heavy snow, heavy rain, strong winds) at the _____ airport. Thank you.

5) Diverted flight

May I have your attention please? We are sorry to announce that Airlines Flight _____from _____ will be diverted due to dense fog (heavy snow, heavy rain, strong winds, a technical problem, a sick passenger). The estimated time of arrival in _____ will be due to dense fog (heavy snow, heavy rain, strong winds). Further information will be announced as soon as possible Thank you.

6) Lost & found

(1) Lost

May I have your attention, please? Any passenger who might have ____ at ____, please turn it in at ____ Airlines information counter. Thank you.

(2) Found

May I have your attention, please? ____ has been found and we would like to return it to its rightful owner. The passenger who lost it, please come to the ____ Airlines information counter. Thank you.

Part II

Tourism English

Tourism English

Unit 01 At The Travel Bureau

Dialog 1

A : Guest, B : Clerk

A : I want to travel to Beijing by air.

B : Yes. When do you wish to go?

A : Next Friday, please.

B : Yes, sir. Do you want to travel by the economy class or first class, sir?

A : How much is it by the economy class?

B : 200 dollars.

A : Could you tell me the time of the flight, please?

B : There's a flight leaving here at 11 : 30 a.m. on Wednesday, arriving in Beijing at 1 : 30 p.m.

A : Is it a jet plane?

B : Yes, it is, sir.

A : That sounds fine.
I'd like to book a seat on the plane.

B : Yes, sir. I'll telephone the airline and ask for a reservation, and I'll leave a note in your box.

A : Thank you very much.

Dialog 2

A : Guest, B : Clerk

A : Good morning.

B : Good morning, sir. Can I help you?

A : Do you arrange sightseeing tours of the city, please?

B : Yes, there's a tour every afternoon, sir, leaving here at two o'clock.
The price is 40,000 won.
I'm sure you'd find it very enjoyable.

A : Then I'll book two seats for this afternoon.

B : Yes, sir. That will be 80,000 won, please.

A : Thanks a lot.

Dialog 3

A : Clerk, B : Guest

A : Good evening. May I help you, sir?

B : I'd like to go to London.
What type of flight do you have?

A : We have all kinds of flights.
What day would you like to leave?

B : Well, I'd like to leave on May 1st.

A : Would you like to go on first class or economy class?

B : Economy class, please.

Unit · 02 Informations For Tour

Dialog 1

A : Tourist, B : Clerk

A : Where can I get a map of the subway lines?

B : Here's one for you, sir.

A : How much is it?

B : It's free of charge, sir. Compliments of the hotel. Everybody can have one of each.

A : My wife and I want to hire English-speaking guide for today.

B : Very well, sir. Please fill in this form.

A : What time will the guide come here?

B : Could you wait for an hour or two?

A : Sure.

Dialog 2

A : Tourist, B : Clerk

A : I'd like to take a look around the city this evening. Can I get a ticket for the sightseeing bus?

B : I'm sure you can, sir.

A : What night tours do they have?

B : They have many, sir.
Just take "This Week in Seoul" with you, and choose the tour you'd like best.

A : Oh, thank you. I'd like to take Tour B.
Where can I catch the bus?

B : Take the bus in front of this hotel.

A : Thanks a lot.

Dialog 3

A : Tourist, B : Policeman, C : Passer-by

A : I beg your pardon, can you tell me how to get to the Pagoda Park?

C : I'm sorry, I'm a stranger around here.
That police officer will be able to help you.

A : May I ask you the way to Pagoda Park?

B : I think you'd better take the bus. Get on bus No. 134 or No. 37 at the bus stop over there.

A : How long will it take?

B : I guess it will take about 15 minutes.
It's quite a few blocks from here.

A : Thanks a lot.

B : You are welcome.

Unit 03 On The Street

Dialog 1

A : Tourist, B : Passer-by

A : Excuse me, but could you please tell me the way to the American Embassy?

B : Go down this street and turn to the left at the second corner, please.

A : How long will it take me to get there?

B : It's about 15 minutes' walk.

A : Thank you very much.

B : Not at all. You can't miss it.

Dialog 2

A : Tourist, B : Driver

A : Hey, taxi!

B : Where to, sir?

A : I'd like to go to Korea Hotel.

B : Yes, sir. Is this your first visit here?

A : Yes, I've long been looking forward to coming to Korea.

B : Excuse me, but may I ask where you are from?

A : San Francisco, U.S.A.

B : I see.

A : What's the name of this bridge that we're entering?

B : It's the Han-Gang Bridge. Now, we're in Seoul. What do you think of it?

A : Very beautiful city, I think.

B : Here we are. You may get off here, sir.

A : Thank you. Nice to talk to you.
How much do I owe you?

B : ₩25,000, please.

A : Here you are. Keep the change.

B : Thank you, sir.
I hope you'll enjoy your stay in Korea.

A : Thank you. I'm sure I will.

Dialog 3

A : Tourist, B : Passer-by

A : Excuse me, sir.

B : May I help you?

A : How can I get to the pharmacy?

B : Go straight three blocks and turn left.
It's on the second block on your right.

A : Go straight and turn left at the third block, right?

B : And there's a big flower shop at the corner.

B : Next to the shop is the pharmacy.

A : Thank you, sir. Is it far from here?

B : It's ten minutes' walk.

Unit · 04 On The Train

Dialog 1

A : Mr. Kim, B : Mr. Golden

A : Do you like traveling on a train?

B : Yes, I like it very much.

A : Have you ever taken a long journey by train?

B : Yes, I once traveled from New York to Seattle.

A : How long did it take you to do the journey?

B : Nearly three days and nights.
That was on the streamliner.
It takes longer on regular trains.

A : What kind of trains are there?

B : The streamliners are diesel driven. Most of the trains are run by diesel, though. Electrically driven trains are used in the high mountains and on local runs around the suburbs of the big cities.

A : Are the American train cars like the Korean?

B : In construction, yes, what we call a day coach is similar. But, due to the long trip, many of the coaches have reclining seats which are very comfortable for sleeping.

Dialog 2

A : Mr. Kim, B : Mr. Golden

A : Are there other types of cars?

B : Yes, the sleeping car which we call a Pullman.

A : Are American trains always on time?

B : In winter they are often slowed down by snow, and in general not as punctual as they should be.

A : What classes are there on your trains?

B : Usually just two, Pullman and day coach.

A : Who's the man that checks the ticket?

B : He is the conductor. There are also an engineer who runs the train and porters who help you with your baggage.

Dialog 3

A : Mr. Kim, B : Mr. Golden

B : Excuse me, but is this Seat No. 32?

A : Yes, right here.

B : Thank you.

A : How far are you going?

B : As far as Gyeongju.

A : Oh, are you? That's where I'm going, too.

B : That's good. I'm glad to meet you.

A : Are you going to do the sights of Gyeongju?

B : Yes, I'd like to see Busan, too.

A : How long are you going to stay in Gyeongju?

B : About a week. My name is Thomas Golden. And you?

A : My name is Kim, Mee yeon, Kim is my surname.

Unit 05 At The Bank

Dialog 1

A : Tourist, B : Information Clerk

A : Where can I cash some traveler's checks?

B : Please go to the third window.

A : Thank you.

B : It's my pleasure.

Dialog 2

A : Tourist, B : Teller

A : Would you cash this $50 check please?

B : Certainly. How would you like it?

A : Well, I'd like one twenty, two tens, one five, and five ones.

B : All right, sir. Here you are. Twenty, thirty, forty, forty-five, forty-six, forty-seven, forty-eight, forty-nine, and fifty. Would you check it please?

A : Yes, I'd like to.

B : Thank you, sir.

Dialog 3

A : Tourist, B : Teller

A : Could you exchange these American dollars into Korean money?

B : Yes, sir. How much do you have?

A : $100.

B : All right.

A : What is the current exchange rate?

B : One dollar equals 1,100 won.

A : It has changed, hasn't it?

B : Yes, it has. The American dollar is still going up.

A : Is that right? That's good for me.

B : Here it is, 100,000 won, sir.

A : Well, I think there is a mistake in your calculations.

B : What? Oh, sorry.
I have to pay you 10,000 more won.

A : Right. That is correct.

B : Thank you, sir.

A : Thanks.

Dialog 4

A : Bank Clerk, B : Mr. Park

A : May I help you?

B : Yes, please. I'd like to open a checking account.

A : Fine. Will you fill out this form, please?

B : Certainly.

A : How much are you going to put in your account today?

B : I'll take $1,500 out of my savings account and put it in the checking account.

A : All right. Will this be a joint checking account?

B : I'm sorry. I don't understand what you mean.

A : Are you married?

B : Yes, I am. Why do you ask?

A : Well, do you want your wife to be able to write checks, too?

B : I don't know. I haven't thought about that.

A : Most couples today have joint checking accounts.

B : Well, okay. You can put my wife's name down, too.

A : Certainly.

B : How much do you charge per check?

A : Nothing if you keep a minimum balance of $300 in your account.

B : I hope we can do that.

Unit 06 At The Travel Agency

Dialog 1

A : Tourist, B : Clerk

A : I was thinking of going to Europe.
What type of flight do you have?

B : Where would you like to go?

A : I'd like to go to Paris.
I was thinking of staying in Paris for a while.

B : We have all kinds of flights.
What day would you like to leave?

A : Well, I'd like to leave on March 20th, if I can.

Dialog 2

A : Tourist, B : Clerk

B : Would you like to go on first class or economy class?

A : I'd like to go on economy, of course.

B : O.K. I'll check it. Well, there isn't any on economy.

A : Oh, yeah?

B : I recommend going by Northwest Orient flight.
This one is not too expensive.

A : Do you know if a seat is available?

B : Yes, there is.

A : O.K. I'll take this flight then.

Unit 07 At The Department Store

Dialog 1

A : Sales Girl, B : Tourist

A : May I help you?

B : Yes, please show me that doll.

A : This one?

B : Yes.

A : This will make a good souvenir.

B : What is this made of?

A : The head is made of stainless steel and the body is made of wood.

B : It is really interesting. How much is it?

A : Seven thousand won, sir.

Dialog 2

A : Sales Girl, B : Tourist

B : How much is that bigger one?

A : Twenty thousand won, sir.

B : Well, twenty thousand won.

That's a little expensive for me.

Would you make it cheaper?

A : I'm afraid not, but if you take two dolls...

B : No, I don't want two.

A : Then, I can't.

B : Well, O.K. I'll take that small one.

A : All right, sir. Five thousand won, please.

Dialog 3

A : Tourist, B : Information Girl

A : Excuse me. Where is the men's clothing section?

B : 4th floor, sir.

A : I see, but it is too crowded.

B : Well, then why don't you take the escalator?

A : Yes, but I don't know where it is.

B : Well, you have to go all the way down there and turn to the right.

A : Thank you so much.

Oh, one more thing.

Is there a women's clothing section there, too?

B : No, sir. There is one on the second floor in the new building.

A : Can I go there from here straight?

B : Yes, you can.

A : And you have a food section in the basement, right?

B : I'm sorry, we don't.

A : Oh, yeah. Well, O.K. Thank you very much.

Unit • 08 Talking About Sightseeing

Dialog 1

A : Mr. Kim, B : Mr. Cook

A : What kind of places would you like to visit?

B : I'd like to see Korean things around Seoul and Jeju-Island.

A : Then, Jeju-Island and Seorak Mountain are the best places.

B : Is that right? I want to see Jeju-Island, too.

A : By the way, Thomas, what are you going to do tomorrow?

B : I'd like to do the sights of Seoul.

A : I'll show you around Seoul, then.

B : That's very kind of you.

A : The pleasure is mine.

Well, have you ever travelled by ship?

B : Never. I've seen it in a Korea guide book.

Dialog 2

A : Mr. Kim, B : Mr. Cook

A : Oh, it's nine o'clock already.
I'm afraid I've stayed too late.

B : Do you have to go so soon?

A : Thank you very much for the pleasant evening.

B : You're welcome. We had a good time, too.

B : Must you go already?

A : Yes, thank you very much for inviting me.

B : Please come and see us again soon.

A : Thank you, I will see you tomorrow.
Good night, Mr. Cook.

B : Good night, John.

Dialog 3

A : Tourist, B : Guide

A : Our bus is leaving in a few minutes, isn't it?

B : Right. Do you have tickets with you?

A : Of course, two tickets. One for me, and one for you.
Here, take this ticket.

B : Thank you for your trouble.

A : No, problem.

B : Here comes the bus!

A : Is this the right bus for Sokcho?

B : Look! It says "For Sokcho." Let's take it.

Dialog 4

A : Tourist, B : Guide

[Announcement] "Good morning ladies and gentlemen! We wish to welcome you aboard this bus. We've just left Garngnam Terminal and are now en route to Gangneung, Daegwalyong, as far as Sokcho. We expect to arrive at Sokcho Terminal at 2 p.m. We wish you enjoy your trip. Thank you."

A : I feel like a carsick. Are you all right?

B : Did you suffer from carsick?

A : Yes, sometimes.

Have you any medicine good for carsickness?

B : Here it is. Have some sleep, that'll do you good.

A : Look! There, many farms, here and there.

B : Yes, many.

A : What would you have, tea or coffee?

B : Tea, please.

A : I'll have coffee, please.

B : It's a fine day, isn't it?

Dialog 5

A : Guide, B : Tourist

[Announcement] "Ladies and gentlemen. we'll be arrving at Sokcho Terminal very soon. Attention please. Remain seated until the bus has come to a standstill. We hope you've enjoyed your trip, and that you will take trip with us again. Thank you."

A : We are in Sokcho finally. Did you enjoy your trip?

B : Sure. I did.

A : Is that right. I'm glad to hear that.

Dialog 6

A : Guide, B : Tourist

A : This is the National Park, Mt. Seorak.
There are many tourist attraction.

B : How nice! Will you take me there now?

A : Of course.

B : Oh, what a wonderful waterfall!

A : It's indeed a magnificent sight.

B : How high is that?

A : It's at least 120 feet high.

B : Is that right? Well, what do you call this waterfall?

A : We call it "Biryong".

B : It means "Flying-Dragon."
The weather is too beautiful, I feel as if I were in Eden.

A : Right! Me, too.

Dialog 7

A : Tourist, B : Guide

A : Now, where are you going to take me?
What's the next course?

B : Let's call it a day. You look tired, aren't you?

A : I think so. And you?

B : Me, too.
How about going to the hotel and taking a rest?

A : That's a good idea. Oh, look! The slope road is coming in sight. And the air is getting more and more refreshing, isn't it?

B : Yes, this is over 3,000 feet above sea level.

Dialog 8

A : Tourist, B : Guide

A : What's the name of that high peak?

B : It's Daechong Peak, top of Mt. Seorak.

A : Sure? How high is it?

B : It's over 1,700m above sea level.
Now, let's go to downtown.

A : Yes, Mr. Kim.

Dialog 9

A : Guide, B : Tourist

A : Is this your first visit to Gyeongju?

B : Yes, that's right, Mr. Kim.
I'm so happy that you're going to be my guide.
Isn't Gyeongju your hometown?

A : Yes, I know my way around pretty well.

B : What do you recommend for me to see in Gyeongju?

A : Gyeongju is the home of old Korean fine arts and so you can see many kinds of ancient treasures. You should enjoy here.

B : I imagine that the ancient temples are the most outstanding features of this old capital.

A : Yes, they all offer much in the way of historical interest.

Dialog 10

A : Guide, B : Tourist

A : Here we are at Bulguksa Temple.
Isn't the view from here simply breathtaking?

B : It certainly is.
I never expected to find such a magnificent temple in the middle of this mountain.

B : Is Seokguram Grotto really a cave?

A : Yes. In the center of the cave we can find a large image of Buddha more than five meters high. On the wall, there are beautiful and lively images of Buddha and the Giant.

B : After we have taken in Seokguram Grotto, will we see all the places of importance?

A : It's impossible to see everything in such a short period of time.

B : Why does Gyeongju have so many historical attractions?

A : Because Gyeongju had been the capital of the Silla Kingdom for more than ten centuries.

Dialog 11

A : Guide, B : Tourist

A : This is the famous Bulguksa Temple.

B : It's a very interesting place, isn't it?
Well, this stone is too heavy to lift.
How did they build?

A : It's a surprise to me, too. I have no idea.
Let's go inside.

B : That's the house of worship, isn't it?
What a huge wooden building!

A : Yes, it's quite symmetrical and beautiful.
Here's Daewungjon, what we call.

B : Look at those lotus blossoms.
How beautiful they are!

A : The Bulguksa Temple as also famous for its beautiful gardens and ponds.

B : Are there many temples in this area?

A : Yes, more than fifty.

B : A lot of temples!

A : Sure. And famous museum, and many old mounds.
How about Gyeongju?

B : This view alone is indeed worth coming all the way to Korea to see.

A : I'm glad to here that.

Dialog 12

A : Tourist, B : Guide

A : Oh! What a big waterfall! Have you seen like that?

B : No, I haven't. It's Cheonjeyeon Falls, I hear.

A : Do you remember Niagara Falls?

B : Yes, I've got a very fine tour. How high is it?

A : Well, I can't remember it.

B : What do you think about Nature?

A : Nature? I love it. Nature is life, and life is real.

B : Certainly! As the golden saying goes, "God made the country, and men made the town." you know.

Dialog 13

A : Tourist, B : Guide

A : Why!
How did you know that golden saying, Mr. Kim?

B : I read it in a book.
Haven't you ever heard of Yongduam?

A : I've never heard of it. What's it famous for?

B : It's a rock. It's a dragon head, I mean.
The rock looks like a dragon's head.

A : You mean Dragon Peak?

B : Right! By the way, how did you know it?

A : Nothing. I read it in a guide book.

Dialog 14

A : Tourist, B : Guide

A : We must take lots of pictures.

B : Jeju has some of the most beautiful women in Korea.

A : Where's your camera?

B : Here, I have it. How about having lunch?

A : Let's go and eat.

B : Let's have something special.

Dialog 15

A : Guide, B : Tourist

A : We've arrived in Jeju, at last.
Well, where shall we go first?

B : Look at the sea-bed. It's so clear and blue.

A : Certainly it is! You can see clearly the bottom.

B : It's like an island country, isn't it?
We must take lots of pictures.

A : Jeju has some of the most beautiful women in

Korea. Just look over there.

This's a beautiful island, isn't it?

Where's your camera?

B : Yes, I have.

It's a perfect day for a sightseeing, I think.

A : Where are you going, may I ask?

B : I'm going to Seogwipo, Jeongbang, and Cheonjeyeon Waterfall.

A : Is it your first visit here?

B : Right. Well.... How come did you know that?

A : I'm ready for whatever tourists want.

I'll take you there, if you are all right.

Dialog 16 A : Tour Escort, B : Representative of Local Travel Agent

(Over the telephone)

A : I'd like to talk to you about our group's sightseeing program for tomorrow.

Could you come to our hotel this evening?

B : Be glad to. And when and where in your hotel?

A : At six in the evening in the lobby of Hyatt Regency Hotel.

Is that all right with you?

B : Certainly. (Around 6 p.m. in the lobby of Hyatt Regency Hotel)

B : Excuse me, are you Mr. Kim of Korea Tours?
I am James Jones of Pell Tours in Washington D.C.

A : That's right. Nice to meet you, Mr. Jones.

B : Glad to meet you, Mr. Kim.

A : Let's sit over there and go over the sightseeing program.

B : Yes. (showing a copy of tour itinerary to Mr. Kim)
This is a full-day's excursion to Williamsburg(from Washington).
You'll leave here at 8 : 30 in the morning and will return around 6, just before dinner time.

A : Fine. How far is it from here to Williamsburg?

B : Roughly 200 miles.

Dialog 17

A : Tour conductor, B : Tour guide

A : It's a long drive. Do we stop over somewhere on the way to Williamsburg?

B : Yes, you'll have a rest stop at Fredrickburg some 50 miles from here.
Then, continue for another 80 miles to Richmond.

At Richmond you'll visit the Phillip Morris Cigarette Plant.

I'm sure it'll be an interesting experience for your group, even for non-smokers.

A : How long do we stay in the plant?

B : About an hour or so.

A : Sounds interesting. What about lunch?

Do we eat lunch in Richmond?

B : Yes, just after the plant visit.

We recommend the "Miller Restaurant."

It's a clean and inexpensive seafood restaurant.

It's only a few minutes ride from the plant.

A : Your voucher says, "no lunch is included" in your arrangements.

In other words, we'll have to pay the "Miller" direct, won't we?

B : Yes, that's right.

Dialog 18

A : Tour conductor, B : Tour guide

A : Do we have to reserve tables at the "Miller"?

B : I don't think so. Since you have only 12 members, we have arranged for you to start eating at 1 : 30

p.m. so the restaurant service will not be rushed. It's off the peak lunch hour.

A : Fine. What can we see in Williamsburg?

B : Well, as shown in the itinerary you'll see the Governor's Palace, the Colonial Capital, the Public Gaol, Craft Shops and the National Wax Museum.

A : The admission fees for those places are not included in your tour fare, are they?

B : No, they're not. You settle your account with these establishments yourself.

A : Very well. Can you have our bus park at the hotel at 8 : 20 tomorrow morning?

B : Yes, we can.

Dialog 19

A : Tour Escort, B : Guide

(At Hyatt Regency Hotel on the morning of the sightseeing day)

B : I'm the driver and guide. I work for Bell Tours. My name is Sam Lima. Glad to meet you.

A : Nice meeting you, Mr. Lima. My name is Kim, the tour escort of this Korean group.
Where can I see our bus?

B : It's in the garage of this hotel.

A : Good. Mr. Lima, we'll leave here at 8 : 30.

B : Right. We have ten more minutes to go.
Do your members speak English?

A : No, not all of them. There is a language barrier. They may get what you say when you speak slowly. I'll tell them in Korean what you have said.

B : Good. We'll have an afternoon sightseeing tour in Williamsburg. In the morning I'll tell you all about the colonial days in this country on the way to Williamsburg. It's about four hours ride from here.

A : That'll be an interesting lecture tour for us. When you are talking about historical items, don't try to cover too much. Please pause for a few minutes in between so I can easily translate into Korean. Can you do that?

B : Yes, I can.

A : Can you jot down for me the years when you talk about the important historical events?

B : Sure, I can.

A : Everyone's here now. We can start now.

Dialog 20

A : Tour Escort, B : Guide

B : We are now southern end of Williamsburg.
We'll visit the Information Center to see an outline map of Williamsburg.

A : What else can we study at the Information Center?

B : You can obtain an Official Guidebook.
You can also see a free orientation film in Korean?

A : In Korean?

B : Yes, the orientation is taped in six languages including Korean.

A : Now, we'll get off the bus to see the Center.

B : Bus will be locked, but please don't leave any of your belongings in the bus.

A : No, we won't.
(In the Information Center)

B : Here is an outline map of Williamsburg. We are here now in the Center. I'll mark the places where our bus stops. First, we go anticlockwise on Nicolson Street to the Public Gaol.

A : What the Public Gaol?

B : It's a sort of jail. In 1718. Blackbeard's Pirates were captured and imprisoned here before being hanged.

In Colonial days, debtors and criminals were confined here.

Dialog 21

A : Tour Escort, B : Guide

A : What will we see next?

B : The Capitol. The Capitol is located within walking distance from the Gaol. You will walk down there. No vehicles are allowed to park around there. In ten minutes I'll have the bus turned out there.

A : I got it. When will we visit the Governor's Palace?

B : We'll see the Palace at the end of the tour in Williamsburg. The places we'll see next are the Magazine and National Wax Museum. There again, in twenty minutes the bus will be there to pick you up.

A : Very well.

B : Our tour in Williamsburg will end at the Governor's Palace, which once served as a residence of the royal governors. There are extensive formal gardens and dependencies.

Dialog 22

A : Tour Escort, B : Guide

A : Do we have time for a brief sightseeing of the craftshops?

B : Yes, the bus will pass by the streets that are lined with a variety of craftshops including that of a cabinetmaker, wigmaker, blacksmith, silversmith, gunsmith, harnessmaker, baker, basketmaker, cooper, galt apothecary, jeweler and clockmaker, printer and bookbinder. I think that'll be all for this town.

A : What's galt apothecary?

B : It's the colonial drugstore.

A : I see. Now, how much time did you say will be spent in this Center?
About one hour, right?

B : I think it's enough including the time for watching the orientation film.
Now, you can see the cafeteria over there.
Rest rooms are on the left side of the lobby.
Then I'll see you at 2 : 30 right here.

A : Very well, see you later.

Unit 09 Downtown Seoul

Dialog 1

A : Guide, B : John Smith

A : It's a fine day, isn't it?

B : Yes, very nice.

A : I'll act as a guide today, John.
What would you like to see first?

B : I'd like to go up to Mt. Nam-san.

A : That's a good idea. I'll take you there.

B : What's the tower on the top?

B : Oh, it's Seoul Tower.

A : How high is it?

B : Well, about 500 feet hight.

Dialog 2

A : Guide, B : John Smith

A : We're at the crest of the mountain.
Here's a field glass.

B : Just look down there.
That building is the Gyeongbok Palace, isn't it?

A : You're right. Well, how can you find it?

B : In the guide map.

A : It's Gyeongbok Palace. Where's the National Assembly Building, do you know?

B : That's the National Assembly Building in Yeouido, isn't it?
I've seen it in the guidebook.

Dialog 3

A : Guide, B : John Smith

A : Finally here we are. The building you see over there is the City Hall of Seoul.

B : Oh, I see. What's that stone wall?

A : It's Deoksu Palace. That's one of the places worth visiting in Seoul, I think.

B : Would you take me there?

A : Yes, I will. Come with me.
Here we are in the Plaza.

B : These are fine grasses here and there, aren't they?

A : Here's the best place for many people and artists.
Look! They are displaying an art exhibition.

B : It's a lovely place. What a graceful building it is!

A : How about going and seeing another place, if you want?

B : That's good. Well, where to?

A : I'll show you bronze statues in Sejongno and Gwanghwamun. All right?

B : Are you going there, now?
It's good. Show me the way.

Dialog 4

A : Guide, B : John Smith

A : That's the bronze statue of Lee, Soon Shin, a great warrior of the Joseon Dynasty.

B : Oh, I see. is that a famous "Turtle Ship", then?
I mean that in front of him.

A : How did you know that? Why, certainly!

B : I've seen it in the guide book.
It says Turtle Ship's story there.
Is this the business center of Seoul?

Dialog 5

A : Guide, B : John Smith

A : Now, here's the Myeong-dong.
That's the best shopping district in Seoul.

B : Is it? Certainly!
Oh, how beautiful those flowers are!

A : They're roses.

There are more than 100 varieties, I have.

Well, you look a little tired now.

B : Anyway, let's finish here today.

A : Yes, sure. What a nice day today!

Dialog 6

A : Guide, B : John Smith

A : That's the South Gate, and we call it Namdaemun.

B : What a splendid building it is!

A : It's National Treasure No.

1 in Korea. Watch your step!

There are men working around it.

B : This poster says "For Subway," I know.

A : It's the third line.

B : What's that classic building?

A : Classic? Oh, that's Seoul Station. It's too old.

B : What's the name of this street?

A : The name is South Gate Market Street.

Dialog 7

A : Tourist, B : Agent

A : I'd like to go to Sokcho tomorrow morning.

Give me two tickets, please. Round trip.

B : Beg your pardon?

A : Tow tickets to Sokcho.

B : You've got the wrong place.
We have no express bus to Sokcho.
I think you'd better go and get it at Gangnam Terminal.

Dialog 8

A : Tourist, B : Agent

A : What's the fare to Sokcho?

B : Forty five hundred and ten won, please.

A : You mean round trip or one way trip?

B : We've not round trip. One way only.
Well today's over. Would you have tomorrow's?

A : Yes, two tickets, please.

B : Here are your tickets.

Dialog 9

A : Tourist, B : Agent

A : What time is the bus for Sokcho leaving this terminal?

B : The bus starts every 20 minutes all day.

A : Is it a long ride to Sokcho?

B : Yes, it'll take about five hours.
Is it your first visit to Korea?

A : Yes, I arrived here only five days ago.

B : Have a nice trip.

Unit 10 Meeting Service

Dialog 1

A : Tour Conductor, B : Porter

A : Please take these bags and put them on the bus.

B : How many bags do you have?

A : Thirty-two in all. They are the ones all with Korea Travel Service's yellow tags for identification.

B : May I have your claim tags?

A : Here they are.
How many pieces of baggage do you count?

B : I count 31 so far. I couldn't find the 32nd.

A : The last one is that cardboard box by the counter.
That'll make it 32.

B : Exactly. I see Korean characters on the box.

A : Please keep an eye on these bags, I'll check the bus.
I'll be right back.

Dialog 2 A : Tour Conductor, B : Representative from local travel agent

B : Excuse me, but are you Mr. Kim of Korea Tour?
I'm David Smith from Star Travel Agency.

A : Yes, I am. Nice to meet you, Mr. Smith.

B : Welcome to New York.
I'm told you have 33 people. Are they all here?

A : We're one member less.
We are all here 32 people including myself.

B : I see, then where can I see your bags?

A : They'll come out soon, all with yellow tags.

B : That's an excellent idea to handle bags.

A : Can I use the baggage truck?

B : Oh, no, you can't. Only skycaps may handle this.

Dialog 3 A : Tour Conductor, B : Representative from local travel agent

A : Can I have our voucher?

B : Yes, but not here. I'll pass it to you on the bus.

A : Great, thank you.

B : Are you all on board?

A : One of our members is now in the rest room.
Hold the bus for a minute, please.

B : I see. Here is your voucher you told me(before).
Also, you have here 32 copies of your tour itinerary.

A : Thanks a lot, Mr. Smith.

B : As you see batch of voucher has 23 coupons.
Will you please check it?

A : Everything is fixed. No problem.

B : If you have any changes, fill out the reverse side(back side) of the coupon in detail and endorse it, please.

A : We are all here now. Shall we get started?

Dialog 4

A : Tour Conductor, B : Porter, C : Bus line's staff

B : Where can I see your bus?

A : The bus should be here. It's Boston Line's bus.
Isn't that yellow one ours?

B : I don't think so. It's for another party.

A : I'll contact the bus line to see what happened.
Where can I find a pay telephone?

B : Go straight ahead this way.
It's on the corner to the left.
Have you got a dime?
You need a dime for a city call.

A : I've got it. Hello, is this BOSTON Line?
I want to talk to the dispatcher.

C : Dispatcher Brown speaking. May I help you?

A : This is the tour escort of Korea Tour.
We are all here now at the airport waiting for your bus.

C : Please go ahead.

Dialog 5

A : Tour Conductor, C : Bus line's staff

A : I tried to find your bus, but no bus.
Why is there no bus?

C : I didn't know you were coming in on this early flight.
You are expected to arrive by Northwest Flight 205 at 6 this evening.

A : It couldn't be, we are all here anyway.
There must be something wrong on your side.

C : Now, I'll call the bus terminal to send a bus to the airport right away. Can you wait another hour?

A : We can't wait that long.
Our members are very much upset.
What do you say we cancel your bus and take a

limousine bus to Youngs Terminal?

C : If you insist that way, I must agree to cancel the arrangement.

A : Call Hilton Hotel at 3 o'clock this afternoon.
My Name is Kim.
Let us talk about the detail of this discrepancy at that time.

C : Very well, I'll call you at 3. Thank you for calling.

Dialog 6

A : Tour Conductor, B : Limousine's driver

A : Is this the limousine (bus) to Youngs Terminal?

B : Yes, it is. Are you traveling alone?

A : No, we are (traveling) on a group movement of 32 people with baggage.

B : Bring your bags right here, so that I may put them on the bus.

A : Skycaps will bring them here.

B : I see. Twenty dollars per person to the terminal. You pay me now.

A : Here's 640 dollars for 32 people.
Can you give me a receipt of that amount?

B : I'll work it out as soon as we arrive at the terminal and give it to you there.

A : Is the terminal very far from here?

B : No, not very far, say about 30 miles from here. It's about 30 minutes' ride.

A : Here comes the baggage.
Will you load the bags on the bus?

B : (After 30 minutes) We are now approaching Youngs Terminal. Have a nice trip.

A : Thank you, we will.

Unit·11 Reservation For Breakfast

Dialog 1

A : Tour Conductor, B : Head Waiter, C : Waiter

A : I'd like to talk to the head waiter about table reservations for tomorrow morning's breakfast.

C : That would be Mr. Gardner.
Let me check to see if he's in his office.

C : (Some time later) He's in, and he says he'll be right up here in about 5 minutes, sir. Please wait here.

B : Mr. Kim? Welcome to Hyatt Hotel, my Name is Joe Gardner. Glad to see you.

You said something about tomorrow's breakfast?

A : Glad to see you Mr. Gardner, I'd like to make a reservation for 32 people for breakfast tomorrow.

B : Be glad to have you. At what time?

A : At seven.

B : That's a bit early. Waiters do not show up here before 7 : 20 in the morning.

We begin table serving at 7 : 30.

Dialog 2

A : Tour Conductor, B : Head Waiter

A : Then, we'll have our breakfast at 7 : 30. Could you speed up your serving?

We don't have much time in the morning.

B : Very well, then, what will you have for breakfast?

A : Show me the menu, please.

Let me see, we'll have Club Breakfast No. 2.

It'll be fruit juice, scrambled eggs, toast and coffee.

B : Exactly, sir. Any other arrangements?

A : Yes, I'd like to have all the table together.

A : A pitcher of water on each table, and the tables by the windows, if possible.

B : Yes, I could do that.

A : One more thing. Please make out one check and charge it to me. I'll take care of it.

Unit·12 Food Service

Dialog 1

A : Tour Escort, B : Restaurant's Employee

(Making reservations by phone)

A : Hello, Sky Tower Restaurant?
I have a group of 12 people.
We'd like to have dinner at your restaurant around 7 : 30 this evening.
Can you reserve for us good tables near the window commanding a fine view?

B : Twelve people around 7 : 30? We're a bit busy that time. Could you make it at 8?

A : All right, we can. We'll be there at 8. This is Mr. Han, tour escort of Korean Team. Can you have all the tables put together?

B : Yes, we can. Thank you for calling, see you later, sir. (At the restaurant)

B : Good evening Mr. Han. Are all of your people here?

A : Yes, we're all here.

B : Good. May I take your order, sir?
Here is a wine list.
Would you care for some cocktail?

A : Yes, three red Burgundies, two sherries, and 7 beers, please.

B : What brand of beer?

A : What brand do you have?

B : We have Ham, Miller, Schlitz and Bud.

A : Give us Ham, please.

B : Any appetizers that go with the cocktails?

A : Shrimp cocktails for all of us, please.

B : Very well, and soup?

A : Eleven onion soups please.

B : Entrees?

A : Give us a little time to decide.

B : Take your time, sir. (Some time later)

B : Have you decided, sir?

A : Yes, eleven roast beefs and one roast leg of lamb, please.

B : Vegetables?

A : No vegetables.

B : And to follow?

A : We'll decide later.

B : Very well, sir.

A : And for salad twelve hearts of lettuce, please.

B : Very well, sir.
Now may I take your order for dessert?

A : Yes, ten strawberry shortcakes.

B : Beverages?

A : Ten coffees and one milk, please.

B : Yes, sir, thank you very much.

A : And our people drink lots of water.
Can we have pitchers of water on each table?

B : Yes, we'll bring pitchers right away.

Dialog 2

A : Tour Escort, B : Restaurant's Employee

A : Excellent food, delicious.

B : Thank you, sir.

A : Check, please. Make one check and bill it to me.

B : Yes, sir, here it is.

A : How much is it?

B : 360 dollars, sir.

A : Does it include tax and service charge?

B : Yes, all included.

A : Is this Diners Club credit card honored here?

B : Yes, it is (honored).

A : Here you are.

B : May I have your signature here?

A : Certainly.

B : Thank you very much, sir, please come again.

Unit 13 Renting A Car

Dialog 1

A : Korean Traveler, B : Rent-A-Car Office's Staff

B : May I help you?

A : Yes, I'd like to rent a car.
What kind of cars do you have?

B : We have the latest model of Ford and other fine cars.
May I see your driving licence?

A : Yes, here it is. It's an International Driving License.

B : Do you have any identification cards besides this license?

A : I have my passport here.

B : Great, that's the surest thing.

A : Can you tell me the rental charge?

B : The national average daily rate is $10 for 24 hours, plus 15 Cents per mile.

A : What items are included in the rental charge?

B : It includes gas, oil and insurance, regardless of how many rides.

Dialog 2

A : Korean Traveler, B : Rent-A-Car Office's Staff

A : Can you give me any discount for a week rental?

B : Yes, that's averaging $70 plus 15 Cents per mile.

A : Is your rental system carried out on a "rent it here and leave it there" basis?

B : Yes, that's the way we do exactly.

A : Then, may I rent your new Ford for two days?

B : Sure, go easy with your driving and be aware of our traffic that keeps to the right.
Here is your key for the car.
Have a pleasant driving.

A : Thank you, I will.

Dialog 3

A : Korean Traveler, B : Rent-A-Car Office's Staff

A : Could you arrange a rental car for us?

B : Yes, of course, we can.
But only for those participating in the convention.

A : Oh, great. What's the charge?

B : Well, the basic charge for a 2002 BMW is 120 dollars a day and ＄1.5 per running mile.
Tax and insurance are not included.

A : I'd like to rent two Fords for ten o'clock in the morning the day after tomorrow.

B : All right. Will you fill in this form, please?
And you'll have to pay a deposit of thirty dollars per car.
Will you be using a credit card or paying cash?

A : I'll pay cash.
You'll deliver the cars here, won't you?

B : Yes. The cars will be here at the O'Farrell Street entrance the day after tomorrow morning, so pick up your keys at this desk at nine fifty.

A : Where do I turn in the keys?

B : Just turn in the keys here and pay the balance if it's before six in the evening.

Dialog 4

C : Clerk, T : Tourist

C : Good morning, may I help you?

T : Yes, I want to rent a car, please.

C : What type of car are you interested in?

T : A full size sedan.

C : We have the new New EF Sonata.

T : That sounds good.

C : When do you need it?

T : Now. How much is it?

C : Our weekend rate is $70 a day.

C : Would you like limited or unlimited miles?

T : I'd like the unlimited miles.

C : Would you like the optional insurance coverage?

T : No, thanks.

C : May I see your driver's license?

T : I have an International Driver's License.

C : That's fine. How do you want to pay?

T : Visa, please.

C : O.K. Would you sign here, and again here?
Thank you.
Here is your key and the car is right outside.

Dialog 5

C : Clerk, T : Tourist

C : Samson Rent a car. May I help you?

T : Yes, I'd like to rent a compact car tomorrow morning at 9 o'clock for about three days.

C : All right.
We have a Toyota Corolla available for rent.
That's the smallest thing we have right now.

T : That'll be fine. How much do you charge for that?

C : We charge $35.00 per day, but we'll give you 200 free miles a day.
If you run over 600 miles for three days, we'll charge you 25 cents per mile.

T : I see. How about insurance?

C : If you want full insurance, it will be $7.00 per day.

Dialog 6

C : Clerk, T : Tourist

T : I'm here to return the car. The car is right outside.

C : Let me inspect the car.

T : Here's the contract. (Clerk inspects the car.)

C : Everything seems to be fine.

T : I was supposed to bring it yesterday.

C : That's okay, but you will have to pay a late fee.

T : How much is it?

C : One day rental cost.

T : That will be fine.

Unit 14 Phone Call

Dialog 1

A : Mr. Chang, B : Operator, C : Overseas Operator

A : I'd like to make an overseas call to my wife.

B : Yes. Where to, sir?

A : To Seoul, Korea.

B : Hold on, please.
I'll call the overseas operator for you.
(a little later)

C : Hello. This is the overseas operator.
What number do you wish to call?

A : I'd like to make a collect call to Sumi Zo in Seoul, Korea.
Her number is 592-5169.

C : I see.

A : How much time will it take to get through to Seoul?

C : About 10 minutes, sir.

A : Thank you. And what's the toll?

C : It'll be 20 dollars for the first three minutes and an extra 3 dollars for every additional minute, sir.

Dialog 2

A : Operator, B : Mr. Oh, C : Wilson

A : Eagle Audio Supplies. May I help you?

B : Hello. Is Mr. Richard in?

A : I'm sorry, but he is out right now.
May I take a message?

B : Well, then I'd like to speak to Mr. Wilson.

A : Mr. Wilson isn't in this department.
Do you know this extension?

B : I'm afraid not.

A : I'll look it up for you then.
May I ask who's calling?

B : Yes. My name's Mr. Oh.
I'm with an electric company.

A : Will you hold the line, please?

B : Certainly.

C : Hello, Mr. Oh? Sorry to keep you waiting.

B : Oh, hello, Mr. Wilson. Don't worry about it.

C : What can I do for you this morning?

B : Do you have any free time this afternoon or tomorrow?

C : Well it's a pretty busy time of the year for us.
I may be able to spare a few minutes tomorrow afternoon.
Do you think you could make it between 2 : 45 and 3 : 30?

B : I'm sure I could.

C : Fine. See you tomorrow. Thank you for calling.

B : You're welcome. See you tomorrow around 2 : 45.

Unit 15 Going To A Restaurant

Dialog

A : Mr. Martin, B : Mr. Chang

A : What kind of food do you like, Mr. Chang?

B : I like all kinds of food.

A : Oh really? Where would you like to go?

B : I don't know any places around here.

A : I know a great Thai restaurant.
It's only three blocks from here.

B : Oh. Well, I guess we could go there.

A : You don't sound very excited about it.

B : To tell you the truth, I think Thai food is too hot.

A : How about a steakhouse?

B : That sounds better. (in the restaurant)

A : What would you like to drink?

B : I'd like a bottle of beer.

A : How about something to go with the drink?

B : I'll have some peanuts.

A : OK. Now please order anything you like.

B : Thank you very much.

A : Why don't you get a big steak?
I hear beef is very expensive in Korea.

B : It is, and I will!

A : Well, I'll order for both of us.
How would you like your steak?

B : Medium, please.

Unit·16 Public Transportation

Dialog

A : Mrs. Chang, B : Ticket Agent, C : Man In The Street

A : Give me a one-way ticket to New York.

B : Here you are.

That will be twenty-two dollars and a half.

A : Where do I have to change trains?

B : You don't have to, unless you take the local.

A : What time does the next express leave?

B : At 9 : 30. You have plenty of time to catch it.

A : Which platform does the train leave from?

B : From No. 12.

A : Thanks for all your help.

B : Don't mention it. It's a part of my job.

(In New York)

A : Excuse me. Where can I get a taxi?

C : At the bus terminal. It's three blocks over there.

A : Thanks a lot.

Why aren't there any taxis at this train station?

C : I don't know.

Unit 17 Invitations

Dialog

A : Mr. Limb, B : Bill

A : Bill, I'd like to invite you to have dinner with us.

B : Thank you very much. I always look forward to your wife's great Korean cooking.

A : It's nice of you to say so.

B : When will it be?

A : Next Saturday.
We're inviting the Clarks, the Michael and Walker.

B : Sounds like a party—not just dinner.

A : Well you can call it whatever you like.
Just be sure to come.

B : I wouldn't miss it for the world.
I'm playing golf that afternoon until 6 : 00.
What time should I get there?

A : The party is going to start at seven.
Why don't you come over a little after that?

B : That would be fine.

A : And don't eat anything before you come.

B : I'll starve myself all day. You don't have to worry about me not eating enough.

A : Okay. See you Saturday.

B : Thanks again. I'm looking forward to it.

Unit 18 Asking Directions

Dialog

A : Mr Kwon, B : Dweller

A : Excuse me.

B : Yes, can I help you?

A : Where can I find a drugstore around here?

B : Turn left at the corner. There's one a few stores down on your side of the street.

A : On my side of the street?

B : Yes. I mean on this side. You can't miss it.

A : Thank you very much. Is it Walgreen Drugstore?

B : I'm not sure. It's either Walgreen or Rexall.
Is it important?

A : Well. Yes it is.

B : Why? What kind of medicine are you going to buy?

A : Oh, I'm not going to buy any medicine.

B : Then why are you going to the drugstore?

A : I'm hungry. I want to eat at the lunch counter.

B : Well, what difference does it make whether it's a Walgreen drugstore, Rexall drugstore, or any other kind of drugstore?

A : Well, I love the strawberry shortcake at Walgreen's.

B : I hope you find what you're looking for.

A : Thank you for all the help.

Unit•19 At The Post Office

Dialog

A : Postal Clerk, B : Mr. Hong

A : Can I help you?

B : Yes, I'd like to send this by airmail.

A : Where is it going?

B : To Korea.

A : Seoul?

B : No, Inchon.

A : Well, I guess the rate's the same.
What does it contain?

B : It contains magazines.

A : Then you can get the special rate by sending it as printed matter.

B : Oh, is that cheaper?

A : Yes, it is. Quite a bit. You aren't sending it to a school or a library, are you?

B : No. Would that make a difference?

A : Well, sometimes there's a special rate for educational materials.

B : Well, I'm just sending this to a friend.
Actually it contains men's magazines.

A : I see. But you could really call them educational materials, couldn't you?

B : Maybe. But my friend always brags that he knows everything about women already. So I suppose I'm not "educating" him.

Unit 20 At The Pharmacy

Dialog

A : Mr. Kwon, B : Druggist

A : Do you have any medicine for an upset stomach?

B : Yes. We have several kinds.

A : Well, I have a stomachache and I need some medicine.

B : How long have you had the pain?

A : Since yesterday afternoon.
I thought it was something that would just go away.

B : Have you had this kind of trouble before?

A : Yes. But not very often.

B : Have you been to the doctor?

A : No, it's not that serious.
Now do you have any medicine for me?

B : Yes, this one will be good.

A : How much is it?

B : It's three dollars and forty-two cents, including the tax.

A : Okay. Here's a five.

B : There you are. Here's your change.
I hope you feel better soon.

A : Thank you. I'm sure I will.

Part
III

Articles on Tourism

Articles on Tourism

Unit • 01 Tourism Today

The world becoming a global village in which people from different continents are made to feel like next door neighbors. In facilitating more authentic social relationships between individuals, tourism can help overcome many real prejudices, and foster new bonds of fraternity. In this sense tourism has become a real force for world peace.

Pope John Paul II

International tourism in the twenty-first century will be a major vehicle for fulfilling people's aspirations for a higher quality of life, a part of which will be through "facilitating more authentic social relationships between individuals" and, it is hoped, laying the groundwork for a peaceful society through global touristic contacts. International tourism also has the potential to be one of the most important stimulants for global improvement in the social, cultural, economic, political, and ecological dimensions of future lifestyles. Finally, tourism will be a principal factor for creating greater international understanding and good will and a primary ingredient for peace on earth.

As we approach the threshold of the twenty-first century, the dynamic progress that has been made in international tourism will accelerate even more. This phenomenon is resulting from the fact that the last half of the twentieth century is witnessing tremendous technological changes in transportation and communication, the twin engines that are propelling enormous changes in worldwide tourism. While there have been many turbulences, individual conflicts, and outright wars, the world has been fortunate in avoiding a Would War III especially a nuclear conflict, which, in effect, would have destroyed any progress that has been made in tourism. It has been clear in the past, and will be true in the future, that peace and prosperity are the keys that best open the door to tourism growth. In brief, people in the twenty-first century will look to quality international tourism for creating greater happiness and for improving the human and social aspects of life while at the same time providing opportunities for economic development, job creation, and international trade.

Unit 02 Tourism Defined

1) Tourism defined

(1) Tourism : With respect to international tourism, the term tourism is used by the World Tourism Organization as follows :

① The entire world industry of travel, hotels, transportation, and all other components of tourism, including promotion, which serves the needs and wants of travelers. Tourism today is conceived of with a brand new meaning. It is primarily a term of economics referring to an industry.

② To a nation(political sub-division or transportation centered economic areas of contiguous nations), the sum total of tourist expenditures within their borders is referred to as the nation's tourism or tourist industry, it is thus ranked with the national industry. More important than just the total monetary product value of tourism is its role in the balance of trade. Here tourism earning from foreigners truly represents export industry. Tourism is an "invisible export."

③ Tourism is called export industry without a chimney, education without a class room, communication without a press and diplomacy without a protocol.

(2) Visitor : any person visiting a country other than that in which the person usually resides, for any reason other than following an occupation remunerated from within the country visited. This definition covers two classes of visitors : "tourist" and "excursionist."

① **Tourist :** A person who travels from place to place for non-work reasons. By UNWTO definition, a tourist is someone who stays for more than one night and less than a year. Business and convention travel is included. This thinking is dominated by balance of trade concepts. Military persons, diplomats, and resident students are not tourists.

② **Excursionist :** A temporary visitor staying less than twenty-four hours in the country visited (including travelers on cruises).

(3) **Tour :** A long distance circuit of more than 3 days organized by a travel agency in a given town and comprises sightseeing in several other places or towns, either within or outside the country origin.

(4) **Sightseeing :** A tour within the city limits showing clients the main particularities of the place : avenues, churches, monuments etc.

(5) **Excursion :** A tour outside the limits, but however, in the vicinity of the town where the organizing agency is located. Such a tour may last from half a day to three days according to the rule adopted in this tariff. It comprises accommodation, meals and transportation from departure to

return to the given town.

(6) **Voyage :** A relatively long journey or passage by sea or other large body of water or formerly by land.

(7) **Travel :** Travel is the act or action or taking a tour, a journey or a trip(Webster's dictionary : To go from one place to another.) ; "We will travel to Gyongju by bus."

(8) **Trip :** Trip means journey, especially a pleasure excursion. Usually used for a short excursion. In U.S. we say also "I will take a business trip." It is differentiated from tour ; "The KNTO trip to the PATA conference was a huge success."

(9) **Journey :** Journey used mostly with distance travel means to go to a place, especially a distant place usually on land.

ex 1) "He took a long journey of 3 days on the Siberian Railway."
"The journeys of Marco Polo."

ex 2) **PATA conference :** Many hotel managers travel agents and tourism directors will travel to Korea for the PATA conference. Some will tour the country. After they finish the trip(or journey; trip is the better word to use here), some will return to their own countries. Other will go to see Gyeongju. After a long journey to Gyeongju, back to Seoul and then they will travel to Hong Kong by KAL.

(10) Flight

① Of or related to the airborne movement of an aircraft, commonly used as an abbreviated form of scheduled flight.

② Refers to one complete movement from the point of origin to the final destination disregarding stop-overs. A one-way flight is counted as one flight. A round trip flight is considered two flights.

(11) Leisure time : Time that a person does not devote to work or personal maintenance and care.

(12) Play : Free, spontaneous activity; synonymous with recreation. An activity done for its own sake, rather than for economic gain. Tourism may be considered a form of play.

(13) Recreation

① Diverse activities freely chosen excluding those activities connected with work. Commercial recreation is the provision of means for a pleasurable activity for the purpose of making a profit. Public recreation is the provision of similar means, financed and usually managed by a government agency.

② The action and activities of people engaging in constructive and personally pleasurable use of leisure time. Recreation may include passive or active participation in individual or group sports, cultural functions, natural and human history appreciation, non formal education, pleasure travel, sightseeing, and entertainment(National Tourism policy Act, U.S.A)

2) Tourism more broadly defined

The late futurist Herman Kahn, In his book The Next 2000 Years, wrote, "It seems reasonable to assume that by the end of the century tourism will be one of the largest industries in the world, if not the largest." What, then, is tourism? Travel, or tourism, means different things to different people. To many individuals and policymakers, travel or tourism is thought of only as an activity pursued with one's leisure time. It is far broader than that, considerably more complicated, and a very significant segment of the world's economy.

Tourism has strong links to cultural pursuits, foreign policy initiatives, economic development, and provides an opportunity to increase worldwide understanding, mutual goodwill, and peace. The tourism industry includes the buying, selling, and management of services and products (to tourists), which might range from buying hotel rooms to selling souvenirs or managing an airline.

The tourism industry demands the most creative and innovative managers because tourism represents one of the most perishable of the products that exist in the worldwide marketplace. If the hotel rooms, airline seats, or restaurant tables are not filled immediately, they are gone forever—there is no opportunity to put such products in storage or in inventory.

Tourism is also the most wide-ranging industry in the sense that it demands products from other sectors of the economy. For example, the beef and wheat grown in Kansas help feed the international visitors in New York City or Los Angeles. Airplanes must be produced, computer reservation systems developed, and steel and concrete manufactured for hotel construction. The point is that there is no other industry in the economy that is linked to so many diverse and different kinds of products and services as is the tourism industry. In order to plan for and provide rational order to such a diverse and dynamic industry, it is necessary to develop policies to assist the decision makers in this complex industry.

Unit • 03 Domestic Tourism

1) Domestic tourism

When we use the word tourism, we usually think of international travel-people from one country visiting another. However, for most developed nations by far the greatest amount of tourism is generated by people traveling within their own country. This is commonly known as domestic tourism. Domestic travel—although it is more difficult to quantify than is international tourism, because there are no national borders to be crossed at which tourists can be counted—is estimated to be 75 to 80 percent of all tourism activity.

Most domestic tourism is a natural offshoot of changes in life-styles and particularly in the use of the automobile as a means of transport. First came a move away from rural living to urbanization. This urbanization led to families' moving to the suburbs from where they were able to commute to and from work. The growth in incomes also meant more visits to relatives and friends. People increasingly came to perceive vacations as an intrinsic part of their life rather than as a luxury. Finally, the automobile is estimated to be the chosen mode of transportation for more than 75 percent of domestic tourism.

Most governments try to encourage domestic tourism and discourage their own citizens—often through advertising., although sometimes by other means such as currency controls—from going abroad. But sometimes these controls are not necessary, as world economic forces can change monetary values. For example, when world economic conditions force the dollar to drop in regard to foreign currencies, this makes the purchase of those foreign currencies(and thus the cost of foreign tourist vacations that must be paid for in those foreign currencies) more expensive.

2) Local tourism

Even within a country, cities and regions vie with one another to keep their own tourism "local." They also try to increase their share of the total domestic tourism pie, as well as maximize the number of foreign tourists coming to that city, area, or region.

Cities and regions do this by investing in tourism research, planning, and promotion. For example, many cities have tourism and convention bureaus.

Conventions, in particular, can be a major generator of tourism if they are national or international in scope. They bring a great deal of new money into an area to be spent in hotels, restaurants, shops, and attractions and on many other goods and services. This money filters through many levels and greatly benefits the local economy.

Unit 04 International Tourism

Most international travelers come from countries with a relatively high standard of living combined with a high rate of economic growth in which industry and commerce form the base of the economy. Such countries have a high rate of urbanization, in which equality of incomes is part of their social system. The international tourism market is primarily composed of middle -income people who have managerial or professional positions or work in supervisory and skilled jobs.

Exporting goods is one way to earn foreign currency. Another way that is becoming more and more important to most countries is to attract foreign tourists. This form of export is often referred to as an *invisible export*.

- Developing countries -

Invisible exports are also critical to many Third World or developing countries who have no tangible goods to export. These developing countries must rely solely on exporting their tourism to earn the foreign currency they need to import goods to help raise the economic well-being of their citizens. These developing contries generally have few or no domestic tourists and so must depend on foreign tourists to occupy their hotels, eat in their restaurants, and spend money in their shops and on their attractions.

- Balance of trade -

Residents of a country who take a holiday abroad need the currency of the foreign country they plan to visit. In order to buy foreign currency they must spend their own money. From a financial point of view, this is the equivalent of importing goods from abroad. The more money that flows out of a country as a result of its citizens' traveling abroad, the more probable it is that that country will have a travel deficit.

A travel deficit occurs when more of a country's money is spent abroad by its own citizens than is earned by that country from foreigners visiting it. A *travel deficit* is the same as spending more money on imported goods than is earned from exported goods. Thus, it is important for most countries not only to encourage domestic tourism but also to discourage its own citizens from traveling abroad. Economists define this as *import substitution.*

Some people find it difficult to visualize tourists coming into a country as an export for that country ; they usually consider exports to be goods going out of a country. However, tourists coming into a country can be conceptualized as an export by thinking about who receives the money from selling the product. In other words, who is the seller in tourism? The answer is the host country or region. Tourism differs from many other types of export only in that the purchaser "consumes" the goods and services on the seller's premises!

For both political and currency reasons, some countries impose severe restrictions on their citizens' traveling abroad, while still welcoming foreign travelers into their country. This helps ensure that they do not have a travel deficit and also that they have what economists refer to as a *positive balance of trade*. This positive balance of trade occurs when the total earnings from exports of goods and services (which includes foreign travelers coming into the country) are higher than the cost of imported goods and services (which includes its own citizens' going abroad).

Unit 05 International Government Organizations

There are a number of world and regional international organizations, sponsored by national governments and others, that are heavily involved in international tourism.

- UN World Tourism Organization (UNWTO) -

One of the most important international tourism organizations is the World Tourism Organization (WTO), with its headquarters in Madrid, Spain. The WTO represents all national and official tourist interests and is recognized as the official consultative body on tourism to the United Nations. The WTO's basic objective is the promotion and development of tourism with a view to contributing to economic development, international understanding, peace, prosperity, and universal respect for and observance of human rights and fundamental freedom for all without distinction as to race, sex, language, or religion. In achieving this goal the WTO pays particular attention to the interests of the developing countries in the field of tourism and collaborates with appropriate branches of the United Nations and its specialized agencies.

Some of the many ways in which the WTO is involved in tourism are

* Helping developing countries in tourist endeavors.
* Acting as an international clearinghouse for tourist information.
* Encouraging the application of new knowledge to tourism development and marketing.
* Promoting cooperation among all countries in technical matters affecting tourism.
* Harmonizing tourist policies among nations by formulating and applying international tourism principles.
* Standardizing equipment, terms, and signs to aid tourists.
* Recommending positive tourism measures, such as the creation of new tourist facilities.
* Promoting tourism and spreading an appreciation of its advantages.

* Conducting regular surveys of world tourism.
* Creating methods of forecasting, measuring, and marketing tourism that will be of use to national tourist organizations in their own endeavors.
* Encouraging research leading to improvement in the comparability of tourist statistics.
* Facilitating world travel by encouraging the elimination or reduction of government control on international travel and by such means as standardizing passports, visas, and frontier formalities.

- International Civil Aviation Organization (ICAO) -

The International Civil Aviation Organization (ICAO) was formed in 1944 to establish technical agreements for the safety of the airlines, covering such matters as standardizing equipment, training, communication, and security and to foster cooperation among countries on airline matters. The ICAO is also the medium through which agreements are established among countries that wish to exchange airline routes. About eighty countries are members of the ICAO.

- International Air Transport Association (IATA) -

The International Air Transport Association (IATA) was established in 1945 to promote safe, regular, and economical air transport. The IATA's members are individual international airlines.

The IATA acts as a ticket clearinghouse and ensures the standardization of such things as prices, tickets, weigh bills, and baggage checks. The IATA's main role is setting international airfares. Any IATA agreements on fares are not binding on any individual airline until they are ratified by their national governments, which is not normally a problem.

IATA was much more than a fare-fixer : it provided the central machinery—which ICAO could not—to coordinate and synchronise the growing network of air routes. Its timetable conferences connected up flights. Its committees on technology and safety maintained common standards. It invented the remarkable IATA ticket, which was to remain the means not only of booking seats across the world, but of changing airlines and switching currencies. A passenger could buy a multiple ticket in New York or Bangkok, unfolding like a concertina, to carry him on twenty airlines in twenty currencies to twenty destinations. Carbon copies were torn off at each stage, to be sent back to the central IATA clearing-house—an extraordinary feat of global organization and trust.

But not everyone loves the IATA. It was described by one anonymous member as "a cartel that combines privately owned enterprises struggling for survival with state-owned enterprises operated only for nationalistic reasons."

- Organization for Economic Cooperation and Development (OECD) -

The Organization for Economic Cooperation and Development (OECD) was established in 1960 in Paris with the objective of promoting policies that would achieve the highest sustainable economic growth and development and raise the standard of living among its member countries, as well as to contribute to the expansion of the economy and to world trade. Because tourism plays an integral part in achieving these goals, the OECD has a tourism committee for coordinating tourism studies and arranging meetings among member countries to improve statistical methods of monetary exchange and accounting. The OECD also prepares an annual report entitled *Tourism Policy and International Tourism in OECD Member Countries*. Most of the more than twenty OECD members countries are from Europe; other members are Korea, Australia, Canada, Japan, New Zealand, and the United States.

- Organization of American States (OAS) -

The Organization of American States (OAS) has objectives similar to those of the OECD, but it limits its activities to North, Central, and Latin America.

- Pacific Asia Travel Association (PATA) -

The Pacific Asia Travel Association (PATA) was organized in 1951. Although many governments are members, there are more than one thousand other organizations that are nongovernment members. These include airlines, steamship lines, ground transportation companies, travel agents, wholesale tour operators, travel associations, hotels, tourism trade publishers, public relations firms, and advertisers. The major objective of the PATA is to develop, promote, and facilitate travel in the Pacific area, which includes North America. PATA achieves this objective by arranging conferences and seminars, producing publications and reports, and sponsoring training programs.

- American Society of Travel Agents (ASTA) -

The American Society of Trevel Agents was established in 1931. Trade association of the United States travel agents and tour operators. International and allied memberships for trade-associated industries are also offered.

- Other Organizations -

- ✔ **AACVB** : The Asian Association of Convention and Visitor Bureaus was established in 1931.

- **APEC** : The Asia Pacific Economic Cooperation was established in 1989.
- **ASEM** : The Asia Europe Meeting was established 1996.
- **ATMA(EATA)** : The Asia Travel Marketing Association was established in 1966.
- **IACVB** : The International Association of Convention And Visitor Bureaus was established in 1914.
- **ICCA** : The International Congress and Convention Association was established in 1936.
- **TTRA** : The Travel and Tourism Research Association was established in 1970.
- **APTA** : The Asia Pacific Tourism Association was established in 1995(Busan,Korea)
- **ETC** : European Travel Commission
- **CMTA** : Common Market Travel Association
- **CTA** : Caribbean Tourism Association
- **SATO** : South American Tourist Organization

Part
IV

Korea in Brief

Korea in Brief

Unit • 01 History

The habitation of early man in Korea appears to have started about half a million years ago. The first kingdom, named Gojoseon(Ancient Joseon), was formed in 2333 BC. By the first century BC, Korea's three ancient kingdoms of Goguryeo, Baekje and Silla ruled the whole Korean peninsula and much of Manchuria; they were by far the most powerful and eminent kingdoms in the area. The period of their rule, 57 BC-AD 668, is known as the Three Kingdoms period, Goguryeo and Baekje were ultimately vanquished by Silla in 668 and 660 respectively. In 676, Silla unified the peninsula for the first time. The Unified Silla period, 676-935, was a golden age for Korean culture. The advancement in the area of Buddhist art are especially noteworthy.

In the succeeding Goryeo Dynasty, 918-1392, an aristocratic government was instituted. Buddhism was established as the state religion and came to have great influence in the political and administrative spheres. The name "Korea" is a derivative of "Goryeo".

- Dangun and the Founding Myth of Korea

A long time ago when Hwanung, a son of Heaven, ruled the people, there lived a tiger and a bear. They wished whole heartedly to become human and prayed every day to Hwanung to grant their wish. Upon hearing their fervent prayers, Hwanung called them to him and gave them 20 cloves of garlic and a bunch of mugwort, then told them that if they could remain out of the sunlight for 100 days, only eating that food, then he would grant them their wish. The tiger gave up after a little while and left the cave, but the bear remained true and after 21 days, Hwanung transformed the bear into a beautiful woman.

The bear-woman, Ungnyeo was very grateful and made offerings to Hwanung, but arter a while had passed she became sad from being lonley. Once again, she prayed to Hwanung beneath a sandalwood tree, to be blessed with a child. Hwanung, moved by her prayers, took her for his wife and soon she gave birth to a son. They named him Dangun Wanggeom, who later established the Gojoseon (Ancient Joseon Kingdom) in 2333 BC, which was the first kingdom on the Korean peninsula.

The Joseon Dynasty (1392-1910) was the peninsula's final dynasty. During this period, various political and economic reforms were enacted. The most prominent of these was the adoption of Confucianism as the state ideology. The surge of creative literary endeavors and the invention of hangeul(the Korean alphabet) in 1443 invest this period with special city in 1394.

Palaces and gates constructed during this period can still be seen in the city today.

The Japanese invasion of the peninsula in 1910 ended the Joseon Dynasty. Korea remained under Japanese colonial rule for 35 wears until the end of World War II. On August 15, 1945, Japan surrendered to the Allies and withdrew from the Korean Peninsula, which was then divided into two: South korea in the free world and North Korea in the communist bloc. The republic of Korea in the south established an independent government three years later.

The Korean War began on June 25, 1950, when North Korea invaded the South. An armistice agreement was signed three years later in 1953.

South Korea's tireless post-war reconstruction efforts were highly successful in the promotion of national prosperity and stability.

In 1988, Seoul the capital of the South, hosted the Olympics. In September 1991, South and North Korea were simultaneously admitted to the United Nations, then in June 2000, historic summit talks between South and North Korea were held in

Pyeongyang, the capital of the North. The 17th FIFA World Cup was held jointly in 2002 by Korea and Japan, juring which the Korean national team achieved the legendary feat of being the first Asian national team to proceed to the semifinals in the history of the World Cup competition.

Unit • 02 Land

The Korean peninsula extends southward from the eastern end of the Asian continent. Korean peninsula is roughly 1,020km(612miles) long and 175km(105miles) wide at its narrowest point.

Mountains cover 70% of the Korea's land area, making it one of the most mountainous regions in the world.

The lifting and folding of Korea's granite and limestone base has created breathtaking landscapes of scenic hills and valleys. The mountain range that traverses the length of the east coast plunges steeply into the East Sea, while along the southern and western coasts, the mountains descend gradually to the coastal plains that produce the bulk of Korea's agricultural crops, especially rice.

The Korean peninsula is divided just slightly north of the 38th parallel. The democratic Republic of Korea in the south and communist North Korea are separated by a demilitarized zone.

South Korea's 99,500sq. km is populated by 47.9 million people(2000). Administratively, the Republic of Korea consists of nine provinces(do); the capital Seoul; and the six metropolitan cities of Busan, Daegu, Incheon, Gwangju, Daejeon, and Ulsan. In total, there are 72 cities(si) and 91 counties(gun).

* Geographic position—Between 33° and 43° north latitude, and 124° and 131° east longitude(including North Korea)
* Highest mountains in S. Korea—Hallasan on Jeju Island, 1,950 meters(6,400ft); Jirisan, 1,915 meters (6,283ft); and Seoraksan, 1,708 meters(5,604ft)
* Rivers—Nakdonggang, 522 km(313 miles); Hangang. 482 km (289 miles); Geumgang, 396 km (238miles)
* Economic status(2000)—GNI US $455.2 billion; national per capita income US $9.628

Unit • 03 Climate

Korea lies in the temperate zone and has four distinct seasons. In late March or early April, the trees burst into leafy splendor to mark the beginning of spring. Mostly sunny days can be expected from March to May.

During the relatively hot and rainy summer season, the vegetation is lush. By June average temperature is over 20°C(68°F). Monsoon rains usually begin around the end of June and last until mid-to-late July. August is hot.

The coming of autumn in late September brings continental winds and clear, dry weather, making the fall months perhaps the most pleasant time of year. October's vivid golds and vibrant reds create a colorful panorama.

December to February are cold and dry with occasional snow or rain. During the winter months, three or four days of cold weather are often followed by a few warmer days.

Unit 04 Religion

Freedom of religion is fully guaranteed in the Republic of Korea. Korea's traditional religions—Shamanism, Buddhism, and Confucianism—have all played an integral role in the country's socio-cultural development. There are also various minor religions based on various combinations of elements from these traditional religions. Christianity has developed a large following since its introduction in the late 18th century.

Unit • 05 Language

The Korean language, like Hungarian, Turkish, Mongolian, and Finnish, is classified into the Ural-Altaic Language group. Hangeul, the Korean alphabet, is composed of 10 simple vowels and 14 consonants. A group of scholars under the patronage of King Sejong developed this systematic rendition of spoken sound in 1443. It is widely acclaimed by linguists as an ingenious invention.

The chart on the next page presents the Romanization of the 24 hangeul letters. This Romanization is based on the new Romanization system proclaimed in 2000 by the Korean government.

However, because all road signs and information boards that are based on McCune-Reischauer system, the old official Romanization cannot be changed immediately, there might be some coexistence of the two systems through 2005.

For your understanding, major changes are listed below.

1) The previously used diacritical mark breve(˘) and apostrophe(') have disappeared in the new system. For example, the vowels 어, 으, 여, and 의 are romanized as eo, eu, yeo, and ui instead of the erstwhile ŏ, ŭ, yŏ, and ŭi. 인천, 영등포 and 여의도 become Incheon, Yeongdeungpo and Yeouido instead of Inch'ŏn, Yŏngdŭngp'o and Yŏŭido as written in the past.

2) When sounds ㄱ, ㄷ, ㅂ, and ㅈ appear before a vowel, they are transcribed by g, d, b, and j, but for the sake of phonetic consistency they are transcribed by k, t, p and ch, when followed by another consonant or forming the final sound of a word. This means that 부산, 합덕 and 제주 have changed from Pusan, Haptŏk and Cheju to Busan, Hapdeok and Jeju. Don't worry—when Koreans hear foreigners pronounce Pusan or Busan, both sound similar and either way is no problem.
3) ㅋ, ㅌ, ㅍ, and ㅊ are romanized as k, t, p and ch instead of the old k', t', p', and ch'. 태평로, 포항, and 청주 become Taepyeongno, Pohang, and Cheongju instead of T'aep'yŏngno, P'ohang, and Ch'ŏngju.
4) 시 is written si instead of shi. Thus 신라 and 임실 become Silla and Imsil.

Unit 06 Seoul

Seoul has been the center of politics, economy, culture, and transportation of Korea for six centuries since Taejo, the founder of the Joseon Dynasty, moved the capital here in the third year(1394) of his reign. Today one quarter of the nation's population live in Seoul, which serves as the broadband core of all branches of knowledge.

Seoul preserves numerous relics of the Joseon Dynasty : Dongdaemun and Namdaemun Gates; five extant palaces, namely Gyeongbokgung, Changdeokgung, Changgyeonggung, Deoksugung, and Gyeonghuigung; royal tombs, including Hongneung and Seonjeongneung; and Seonggyungwan, the Confucian educational institution. The litany of Seoul's cultural heritage is endless. The city's legacy winds through its labyrinthine alleys.

At the same time, Seoul has risen as a global landmark of modernity, with many must-see attractions : Lotte World, an amusement park; Seoul Tower, the symbol of Seoul, blazing the night through; many parks and museums; department stores and other emporiums; jazz bars, cafes, a casino, etc. These make Seoul a favorite tourist destination where visitors find all the amenities and entertainment they could want.

Unit • 07 Gyeongju

Gyeongju was the capital of the Silla Kingdom for a thousand years, and the valley in which it is situated has a great concentration of historical buildings, temples and artifacts. After Silla unified the peninsula in A.D. 676, the city developed into one of the world's major cultural centers. The area is called a "museum without walls" because of the wealth of historical buildings and treasures to be found there.

Tumuli Park(대릉원), a collection of royal Silla tombs from the Pre-Unification Era, is in the middle of Gyeongju. The park contains 20 of the more than 200 royal tombs to be found in Gyeongju. The Cheonmachong (Heavenly Horse Tomb) was excavated in 1974 and yielded more than 10,000 treasures. These treasures, including a golden crown and a girdle, are in the Gyeongju National Museum. The tomb itself is open for viewing, providing visitors with an opportunity to see how the huge tombs were constructed and how the various items were arranged in them. Visitors to this area should be sure to take the time for a peaceful stroll in this serene park.

Cheomseongdae Observatory(첨성대), the world's earliest known existing observatory, is a 7th century bottle-shaped stone structure admired by archeologists worldwide. The square window facing south in the middle of the structure is believed to have served as an entrance, and was probably reached by a ladder.

Anapji Pond(안압지), located ten minutes' walk from Cheomseongdae, is the place where the Silla royal family relaxed and enjoyed themselves. The pond was temporarily drained in 1974 to reveal a veritable treasure trove of Silla artifacts which are now on display in the Gyeongju National

Museum.

Gyeongju National Museum(경주국립 박물관), a place of compelling interest, preserves much of the Silla heritage, including magnificent gold crowns, pottery, Buddhist artifacts, and stone sculptures. The museum also houses the Divine Bell of King Seongdeok the Great, also referred to as the legendary Emille Bell, one of Asia's largest and most resonant bells—19 tons of bronze standing 11 feet high.

The Site of Bunhwangsa Temple(분황사지) is located twenty minutes' walk from Gyeongju National Museum. Only its 3-level stone brick pagoda is still standing, which was originally nine levels high.

Poseokjeong Watercourse(포석정) is where Silla kings used to hold poetry-reciting and drinking parties. Kings would float wine cups to his statesmen seated around the watercourse made in the shape of an abalone shell.

Bulguksa Temple(불국사) is one of Korea's best known temples, a testimony to both the skill of Silla architects and the depth of Buddhist faith at the time. While most of the wooden buildings have been rebuilt over the centuries, all the stone bridges, stairways and pagodas are original. The temple, originally built in A.D. 535, was enlarged in A.D. 752.

Seokguram Grotto(석굴암) is one of the world's finest Buddha shrines, dating back to the same period as Bulguksa Temple. Surrounded by Bodhisattvas and guardian deities, the serene central statue of Buddha gazes out over the forested hills and across the East Sea to the horizon. The carving of the granite dome of Seokguram was a truly amazing architectural feat. In 1995, Bulguksa Temple and Seokguram Grotto were added to UNESCO's prestigious World Cultural Heritage list.

Bomun Lake Resort(보문단지), east of downtown Gyeongju, has five super-deluxe hotels, a convention center, a casino, extensive shopping and dining facilities, golf courses, an amusement park, pleasure boats, a hot spring, and even a contemporary art museum. Shuttle bus and taxi service connect downtown Gyeongju with the resort area. Much more attractions are scattered around Gyeongju : tombs of kings and generals, the holy Namsan Mountain, Yangdong Folk village, and Oksan Confucian School.

Part V

Others

Others

Unit • 01 Job Interviewing

Dialog 1

A : Question, B : Answer

A : Good afternoon. Can I have your name, please?

B : My name is Sunny Kim.

A : When were you born?

B : I was born on January 21st, 1980.

A : Are you married?

B : No, I am single.

A : What do you do for a living?

B : I am a student.

A : What is your nationality?

B : I'm Korean.

Dialog 2

A : Question, B : Answer

A : What is your major?

B : I specialized in tourism administration.

A : If you enter this company, what section would you

like to work in?

B : I'd like to work as a front cashier.

A : If you were to work for this company, how much do you expect to get a month?

B : Well, that's tough question to answer.
Of course the more, the better.
But I believe that I can get seven hundred and fifty dollars a month.

A : Do you have any question you would like to ask me?

B : May I ask how much the bonuses are?

A : We pay 400% annual bonus. Does this satisfy you?

B : I am perfectly satisfied.

A : How many years have you worked in this field?

B : I've worked for three years in this field.

A : What basic principle do you follow in your life?

B : Do not put off till tomorrow what can be done today.

Dialog 3

A : Question, B : Answer

A : Let me ask you a few questions.
Where do you live?

B : I live in Ansan.

A : And what school are you attending?

B : I attend Korea Hotel & Tourism Technical College.

A : Where is that?

B : I beg your pardon?

A : Where is Korea Hotel & Tourism Technical College located?

B : Oh, it's at 542-4, Gojarn-dong, Ansan-si, sir.

A : And what is your major?

B : I'm majoring in Tourist English Interpretation.

A : Have you ever worked in an office before?

B : Yes, I had a part-time job for two months at Samjin Trading Company.

A : What did you do there?

B : Mostly typing and running errands, sir.

A : Have you ever been overseas?

B : Yes, I've been to the United States.
I have lived in New York for one year.

A : Have you studied English typing?

B : Yes, sir. I have studied English typing.

A : What do you like to do in your spare time?

B : Well, I like reading, and listening to music—especially American folk songs. I play the guitar a little, and I like the movies, too.

A : What do you like best about school?

B : The oral English classes.
We get a lot of chances to speak English.

A : Why did you choose this company?

B : Well, I know that you do a very big international business, so I thought it would be a good place for me to use the experience I've had living overseas.

A : Very glad to have met you. We'll be letting you know the result of the interview sometime next week. Thank you very much for coming.

B : Thank you very much for giving me your time.

A : You're quite welcome. Good-bye.

B : Good-bye.

Dialog 4

A : Question, B : Answer

A : Will you introduce yourself to me?
(Tell me a little about yourself.)

B : (...)

A : What school did you graduate from?

B : I graduated from Korea Hotel & Tourism Technical College.

A : What's your major?

B : My major is Tourism.

A : What have you been doing since graduation?

B : I have been studying for the exam of English Tour Guide.

A : What is your home town famous for?

B : My home town is famous for ...

A : How large is your family?

B : There are three in my family.

A : What does your father do?

B : My father works for ...

A : How many palaces are there in Seoul?

B : There are five palaces in Seoul.

A : What does ASTA stand for?

B : It stands for American Society of Travel Agents.

A : What does C.I.Q. stand for?

B : It means Customs, Immigration and Quarantine, sir.

Unit 02 Self Introduction (Autobiography)

My name is Gildong Hong. I was born in Bundarng in 1980. I am the eldest son of four, having an older sister and two brothers. I lived in Bundang through elementary school and middle school and then in my second year of high school we moved to Seoul. So I transferred to Han-Gang high school in Seoul. Well, at first everything was so different, and I felt a little strange, but I made a lot of new friends and then it didn't seem strange anymore. There was a year between the time I graduated from high school and entered the university, because I failed at my first attempt. But I think it helped me grow up. I then entered the Department of Tourist English Interpretation in Korea Hotel & Tourism Technical College and I am a senior student now. As a hobby, I've been playing Baduk ever since my father taught me in high school. Two years ago I was given Chodan. Also, I like listening to music, especially singing songs to my own playing piano, and I am very interested in traveling. For extra-curricular activities, I am a member of Korean U.N.E.S.C.O. Student Association. In my junior year, I was the leader of the group and I got a lot out of it. Especially I learned about working with people. I like to treat people well, especially foreigners because I think it will be an exciting and rewarding job and offer me good opportunities for career development. I have the ambition of being the manager of a top-class hotel, and want to be the best manager in the best hotel in the world. If you hire me, I'll make my every effort with great pride in the job itself and the company. I'm ready to dedicate myself to the development of your company. I'll always do my best for you.

Thank you.

1) Self-Introduction

I'm pleased to have an opportunity to introduce myself to you. My name is Jo, Yeong Seo. I was born in Asan in 1977. I was born while my father's farm was being built, so people said I was a girl who would bring good luck. I went to Asan girl's high school. I was an active member of the students association, and worked hard for my school. It was a good experience in my life.

2) Family Background

My father is a public official. He is very busy but very attentive and thoughtful person at home. He has little tolerance with injustice. He always tells me how I spend money is more important than how much money I earn.

My mother was a teacher of a junior high school and is a housewife. She likes to read a book in her spare time. She cleans up the house too hard and economizes immoderately. Though I sometimes tell my mother that I don't want to live like her, but I really love her.

My younger brother is really cute and lovely. He is a graduate student. When I come back home late, he comes to the bus stop for me. He says it is not because he is worried about my safety, but my hitting somebody. He is humorous and smart.

3) Motto (Basic principle of my life)

I try to keep to a regular schedule every day. Also not to put off till tomorrow what you can do today. Putting things off just makes it worse later, so even if it's hard at the time, I try to get things done that day and not let them go.

4) Personality

I approach things very enthusiastically, I think, and I don't like to leave something half-done. Once I have made up my mind I accomplish my plans. I don't try to get in front of people and lead them, particularly. I'd rather cooperate with everybody else, and get the job done by working together.

5) Interests and Hobbies

I love traveling, and I travel as much as I can. I've been just about everywhere in Korea. And also I enjoy sports, and I like music very much.

6) My Goals in Life

I've wanted to be involved in being the manager of a top-class hotel ever since I was little. If I pass this interview and am accepted into this company, I'll always do my best for you. I want to be a professional in my field.

Unit 03 Personal History (Resume)

RESUME

Nov. 18. 2002

Name in Full	: Kim Dong-Cheul
Date of Birth	: Nov. 18. 1980
Marital Status	: Single
Permanent Address	: 77 Anyang-dong, Anyang-si, Gyeunggi-Do
Present Address	: 301-305, Bansok Apt. 45 Daechi-dong, Daechi-ku, Seoul
Telephone Number	: 02-783-4598

Education

Feb., 1993	: Graduated from Chosuk Elementary School
Feb., 1996	: Graduated from Chosuk Middle School
Mar., 1997	: Entered Harn-Garng High School
Feb., 1999	: Graduated from the above High School
Mar., 2002	: Entered Department of Tourist English Interpretation, Korea Hotel & Tourism Technical College
Feb., 2003	: Will graduate from the above College

Military Service

Feb., 1999	: Entered the Army as a Private

Feb., 2002 : Discharged from service

Work Experience

July-Sept., 2002 : Had an experience as a clerk on a temporary employee at Korea Hotel

Reward and Punishment

No rewards or punishment received.

I affirm that the above statements are true and correct in every respect.

Unit 04 Hospitality Personnel Guideline

1) Smile

(1) A smile costs nothing but gives much.

(2) It enriches those who give it.

(3) It takes not a moment but the memory of it sometimes lasts forever.

(4) None is so rich or mighty that she can get along without it.

(5) None is so poor but that she cannot be made richer by it.

(6) A smile creates happiness in the home, promotes goodwill

in business, and is the cornerstone of friendship.

(7) It can perk up the weary, bring cheer to the discouraged, sunshine to the sad, and nature's best antidote for trouble.

(8) Yet it cannot be bought, begged, borrowed or stolen for it is something that is of no value to anyone else it is given away.

(9) When people are too tired to give you a smile, give them one of yours.

(10) No one needs a smile so much as she who has none to give.

2) A Guide to Hospitality Industry

- Six Secrets of Successful Hotelmanship -

(1) Always keep an eye on the balance sheet.

(2) Don't promise more than you can deliver—deliver more than you promise.

(3) Select the right personnel.

(4) Use the "Personal Touch" to build loyalty among your guests.

(5) Create a warm and welcoming hotel personality.

(6) Cultivate the right attitude toward your position, your staff and your guests.

3) Personal Services as an Escort

A good escort should be sensitive to the needs of the group, to help form a sense of camaraderie and wellbeing. The following are ten "dos and don'ts" :

- Do -

(1) **Smile** : everyone enjoys its warmth and it is contagious.

(2) Dress appropriately and be immaculately groomed at all times. It helps to reinforce your professionalism and the needed authority over the group.

(3) Be patient. Traveling can be a very difficult adventure to the uninitiated.

(4) `Be prepared to have things go wrong : with a little common sense and patience everything can be overcome.

(5) Be friendly, courteous, calm, and, most of all, positive.

(6) **Be prepared** : research the destinations, hotels, etc.

(7) Study the group so as to gear the trip around their interests.

(8) Protect the sightseeing guides and bus drivers if their tips are not included in the package price by reminding the participants of this facts.

(9) Learn the names of each tour participant.

(10) Be understanding but firm regarding rules, etc.

- Don't -

(1) **Forget they are on vacation** : you are on the job!

(2) **Play favorites** : try to appear to like them all equally.

(3) Develop emotional attachments.

(4) Be patronizing or flippant.

(5) Talk too much or feel you have to be the center of attention.

(6) Recommend stores or restaurants unless you are asked.

(7) Inform them of possible problems beforehand if there is nothing they can do about them anyway. The problem might not materialize and there is no need to upset the group for nothing.

(8) Lie if you do not know something; admit it and find the answer.

(9) Be late for anything.

(10) Drink too much.

4) What does PLEASE mean?

P : Posture should be alert and ready to help.

L : Look and listen when dealing with customers.

E : Expression should be friendly, pleasant and natural.

A : Appearance should be smart and clean, and well-groomed.

S : Speech shows your courtesy and friendliness. Use the customer's name, too.

E : Eagerness to help others with a liking for people means you are doing your job successfully.

부 록

Proverbs

1. Absence makes the heart grow fonder.
2. A thing of beauty is a joy forever. (Keats Endymion)
3. Beauty is only skin-deep.
4. As you make your own bed, so must you lie in it.
   (You must suffer for your own mistakes.)
   Cf. He who lives by the sword will die by the sword.
5. Beggars can't be choosers.
6. Don't look a gift-horse in the mouth.
7. A bird in the hand is worth two in the bush.
8. Birds of a feather flock together.
9. Two wrongs don't make a right.
10. It's a case of the blind leading the blind.
11. In the land of the blind the one-eyed man is king.
12. None are so blind as those who will not see. (stubborn people)
    None are so blind as those who cannot see. (too silly to understand)
13. Blood is thicker than water.
14. You can't get blood from a stone.
    You can't get water from a stone.
15. You can't have it both ways.
16. You can't have your cake and eat it too.

17. Boys will be boys.

18. Brevity is the soul of wit. (Hamlet, 2, ii 90)

19. A burnt child dreads the fire.

20. Let bygones be bygones.

21. Let's bury the hatchet.

22. Too much kindness killed the cat.

23. Curiosity killed the cat.

24. A cat has nine lives.

25. When the cat's away, the mice will play.

26. Charity begins at home.

27. The child is father of the man. (Wordsworth)

28. Christmas comes but once a year.

29. Circumstances alter cases.

30. Cleanliness is next to godliness.

31. Every cloud has a silver lining.

32. It's an ill wind that blows nobody any good.

33. The cobbler should stick to his last.

34. Two's company, three's a crowd.

35. Comparisons are odious.

36. Constant dripping wears away a stone.

37. Too many cooks spoil the broth.

38. Don't count your chickens before they're hatched.

39. Cowards die many times before their deaths.
(Julius Caesar)

40. Creaking doors last the longest.

41. Don't cross your bridges before you come to them.
Cf. To burn your bridges behind you.

42. It's no use crying over spilt milk.

43. It's better to be an old man's darling than a young man's slave.

44. Dead men tell no tales.

45. He who hesitates is lost.

46. Discretion is the better part of valour. (Falstaff)

47. Do as I say, not as I do.
cf. Example is better than precept.

48. Every dog has his day.

49. Give a dog a bad name and hang him.

50. Let sleeping dogs lie.

51. Golden lads and girls all must,
As chimney-sweepers, come to dust.
(Shakespeare: Cymbeline.)

52. The early bird catches the worm.

53. First come, first served.

54. First up, best dressed.

55. Easy come, easy go.

56. You can't eat your cake and keep it too.

57. The (surest) way to a man's heart is through his stomach.

58. Enough is as good as a feast.

59. A change is as good as a holiday. (as a rest)

60. To err is human.
To err is human, to forgive divine.

61. Every man for himself and the devil take the hindmost. (Everyone must look after himself and those who are lazy must come to disaster.)

62. Man is master of his fate.
(Every man is the architect of his own fortune.)

63. Example is better than precept.

64. Practice what you preach.

65. The exception proves the rule.

66. Fair exchange is no robbery.

67. Qui s'excuse, s'accuse.
(=He who excuses himself, accuses himself.)

68. Excess begets excess.

69. That's all my eye. (That's all my eye and Betty Martin.)

70. What the eye doesn't see, the heart doesn't grieve.

71. Fact is stranger than fiction.

72. Truth is stranger than fiction.

73. None but the brave deserves the fair. (Dryden)

74. Faint heart never won fair lady.

75. All's fair in love and war.

76. Familiarity breeds contempt.

77. Like father, like son.

78. He who fights and runs away, lives to fight another day.

79. Fine feathers make fine birds.

80. There are as many good fish in the sea as ever came out.

81. A fool and his money are soon parted.

82. There's no fool like an old fool.

83. A fool's bolt is soon shot.
(A foolish person soon wastes his strength or resources.)

84. Forewarned is forearmed.

85. A friend in need is a friend indeed.

86. It is more blessed to give than to receive.

87. Those who live in glass houses shouldn't throw stones.

88. God helps those who help themselves.

89. All that glitters is not gold.

90. One good turn deserves another.

91. Half a loaf is better than no bread.

92. Handsome is as handsome does.
(A person must be judged according to his actions and not by his appearance.)

93. Art is long, Life is short.

94. More haste, less speed.

95. Make hay while the sun shines.

96. Two heads are better than one.

97. The path to hell is paved with good intentions.

98. There's no place like home.

99. Even Homer (sometimes) nods.

100. Honi soit qui mal y pense.
(Evil to him who thinks evil.)

101. Evil lies in the eye of the beholder.

102. There is honour among thieves.

103. Hope springs eternal in the human breast;
(Man never is, but always to be, blest.) (Pope)

104. Laugh and the world laughs with you;
Weep and you weep alone.

105. An englishman's home is his castle.

106. Where ignorance is bliss, 'tis folly to be wise.

107. In for a penny, in for a pound.

108. He's a Jack of all trades but master of none.

109. Know thyself. (Delphi)
(Know thyself ; presume not God to scan.
The proper study of mankind is man. (Pope))

110. Better late than never.

111. It's too late to shut the stable door after the horse has bolted.

112. The labourer is worthy of his hire.

113. He who laughs last laughs longest.

114. A little learning is a dangerous thing.

115. Least said, soonest mended.

116. Life's not all beer and skittles.

117. We live and learn.

118. Live and let live.

119. Long debts make short friends.

120. It's a long lane that has no turning.

121. Look before you leap.

122. Love is blind.

123. Love makes the world go round.

124. The course of true love never did run smooth.

125. It is better to have loved and lost than never to have loved at all.

126. Lucky at cards, unlucky in love.

127. Manners make the man. (Manners make the man.) Manners make the man.

128. Two heads are better than one.

129. Marry in haste and repent at leisure.

130. One's man meat is another man's poison.

131. Adversity makes strange bedfellows.

132. Necessity makes strange bedfellows.

133. A miss is as good as a mile.

134. Money makes money.

135. Money is the root of all evil.

136. Necessity is the mother of invention.

137. It's never too late to mend.

138. You're never too old to learn. You can't teach an old dog new tricks.

139. Never say die. (Never give up hope. Never despair.)

140. A new broom sweeps clean.

141. Ill news travels fast.
Bad news travels fast.

142. No news is good news.

143. Noblesse oblige. (Nobility has its obligations.)

144. Nothing venture, nothing win.

145. One swallow doesn't make a summer.
(You ought not to form a generalization or an optimistic assumption merely because of one good piece of evidence.)

146. Take care of the pence and the pounds will take care of themselves.

147. You can't be in two places at once.

148. Politeness costs nothing.

149. Practice makes perfect.

150. Practice what you preach.

151. There's no time like the present.

152. Procrastination is the thief of time.

153. Don't put off till tomorrow what you can do today.

154. Prevention is better than cure.

155. Every man has his price.

156. The proof of the pudding is in the eating.

157. A prophet is without honour in his own country.

158. Man proposes, God disposes.

159. You can't put back the clock.

160. The more, the merrier.

161. It takes two to make a quarrel.

162. Ask no questions and you'll be told no lies.

163. Don't poke your nose into other people's business.
(Don't interfere in other people's business.)
Don't interfere with other people.

164. Red at night, a shepherd's delight:
Red in the morning, a shepherd's warning.

165. It never rains but it pours.

166. Misfortunes never come singly.
Troubles never come singly.

167. Rats forsake a sinking ship.

168. Reading makes a full man, conference a ready man, writing an exact man.

169. Revenge is sweet.

170. Vengeance is mine and I shall repay.

171. A rolling stone gathers no moss.

172. Rome wasn't built in a day.

173. When in Rome, do as Rome does.
When in Rome, do as the Romans do.

174. There's no rose without a thorn.

175. It is better to be sure than sorry.
(A bird in the hand is worth two in the bush. No. 7)

176. What's good for the goose is good for the gander.

177. Seeing is believing.

178. They also serve who only stand and wait.

179. Catch not at the shadow and lose the substance.
(In Aesop's fable a dog looks into the water and sees the reflection of the bone in its mouth. The dog then tries to get the reflected bone but, in doing so, loses even the bone which it has.)

180. Out of sight, out of mind.

181. You can't make a silk purse out of a sow's ear.

182. If you sing before breakfast, you'll cry before evening.

183. Don't count your chickens before they're hatched.

184. There's many a slip 'twixt the cup and the lip.

185. There's no smoke without fire.

186. Spare the rod and spoil the child.

187. Speech is silver, silence is golden.

188. The spirit is willing but the flesh is weak.

189. Still waters run deep.

190. A stitch in time saves nine.

191. Strike while the iron is hot.
Make hay while the sun shines. (No. 95)

192. There is but one step from the sublime to the ridiculous.
(Napoleon: 1812 : Du sublime au ridicule il n'y a qu'um pas)

193. Genius to madness is always close allied.
And thin partitions do the walls divide. (Pope)

194. Nothing succeeds like success.

195. Talk of the devil and he is sure to appear.

196. Don't spoil the ship for a ha'porth of tar.

197. Everyone to his own taste.

198. There's no accounting for taste.
(De gustibus non disputandum est.)

199. Give a thief enough rope and he will hang himself.

200. Time flies.

201. Time is the great healer.

202. Time cures all ills.

203. Time marches on. (You can't change the course of history.
or Time flies.
or Changes are inevitable.

204. Time is money.

205. Time and tide wait for no man.

206. Every man to his own trade.

207. Never trouble trouble till trouble troubles you.

208. Let sleeping dogs lie.

209. Many a true word is spoken in jest.

210. There's no fool like an old fool.

211. The truth will prevail.

212. Truth will out.

213. Justice will prevail.

214. Variety is the spice of life.

215. When the wine is in, the wit is out.

216. Virtue is its own reward.

217. Everything comes to those who wait.

218. Actions speak louder than words.

219. Walls have ears.

220. You shouldn't wash your dirty linen in public.

221. Waste not, want not.

222. Wilful waste makes woeful want.

223. A watched pot never boils.

224. Self-preservation is the first law of nature.

225. All's well that ends well.

226. The end justifies the means.

227. Where there's a will, there's a way.

228. It's easy to be wise after the event.

229. Sticks and stones will break my bones.
But names will never hurt me.

230. A woman's work is never done.

231. Wonders never cease.

232. It takes all kinds to make a world.

233. One half of the world doesn't know how the other half lives.
(1531 : Rabelais : La moitie du monde ne scait comment l'autre vit.)

234. All work and no play makes Jack a dull boy.

235. Even a worm will turn.

236. If you want a thing well done, do it yourself.

237. Between two stools you always fall.

238. A nod is as good as a wink to a blind horse.

239. A word to the wise is enough.

240. Better safe than sorry.

241. If you can't beat them, join them.

242. A bad work.man quarrels with his tools.

243. If you born poor, It's not your mistake, but if you die poor, It's your mistake.

244. You don't have to win every argument, agree to disagree.

245. Get outside everyday miracles are waiting everywhere.

246. Live your life and forget your age.

247. Don't make decisions when you are angry.

248. Don't pay a job until it is finished.

249. Be careful of those who have nothing to lose.

250. Don't be afraid of saying, "I don't know" or "I am sorry".

251. Look into the eyes of people.

252. Treat every one as you would like to be treated.

253. Learn to listen. It is an art.

254. Enjoy the beauty of this Earth all around you.

255. You have a right to be happy!

256. Health is everything.

257. Confidence is the key to success.

258. In study, it's not the lack of time, but lack of effort.

저자: 임 주 환

현재	순천향대학교 명예교수 한국관광연구학회 고문
	경북대사대부속중학교 졸업 경북고등학교 졸업 고려대학교 법과대학 졸업(학사) 호주 시드니 테크니컬 칼리지 관광과 2년 수료 미국 예일대학 국제회의 관리과정 수료 독일 뮌헨대학 관광문제연구소 관광지개발계획과정 수료 서울대학교 행정대학원 졸업(석사) 한양대학교 대학원 관광학과 졸업(박사)
한국 관광 공사 32년 근속	‣ 진흥처장(해외지사 진흥업무 관장) ‣ 국제회의처장(각종 국제회의 유치 및 행사) ‣ 교육원장(서울교육원장: 통역안내원 및 관광종사원) (경주교육원장: 조리사 및 호텔종사원 양성) ‣ 사업처장(공항 및 항구소재 면세점 관장) ‣ 동남아 지사장(싱가포르 주재: 싱가포르, 말레이시아, 인도네시아, 필리핀, 태국, 브루나이, 인도, 스리랑카 등 관장) ‣ 로스앤젤레스 지사장(미국, 캐나다, 남미, 브라질 등 관장) ‣ 본부장: 부사장(진흥, 사업, 국민관광, 제주개발) ‣ 독일 서베를린 제21회 ITB, 황금의 기수상(Golden, Helm: 관광분야 노벨상이라 함) 수상('87.3.) ‣ 관광의 날 한국관광진흥의 공로로 대통령표창 수상
	경기대, 경희대, 한양대 관광학과 강사 세종대, 단국대, 경희대 대학원 관광 관련학과 강사 순천향대학교 교수 ‣ 관광학과 학과장(충청남도 정책자문교수) ‣ 사회교육본부장(평생교육원, 어학교육원, 컴퓨터교육원) ‣ 충청남도 정책자문교수 디스-관광정보연구원장 2014년 제18대 성남명예시장 위촉
저서	관광정책론, 항공영어, 관광지개발론, 식음료해설론, 신관광법규론, 지속가능한 관광개발, 신관광학의 이해, 관광여행영어
논문	한국의 보전적 관광개발에 관한 한 연구 1990년 대한민국의 정부관광기구(NTO)의 역할 등
자격증	관광통역안내사자격증(영어), 호텔관리사자격증, 다문화가정상담사자격증

Tourism English for Traveling

2006년 9월 10일 초 판 1쇄 발행
2019년 5월 30일 제4판 1쇄 발행

지은이 Limb, Joo-Hwan
펴낸이 진욱상
펴낸곳 백산출판사
교 정 편집부
본문디자인 이문희
표지디자인 오정은

등 록 1974년 1월 9일 제406-1974-000001호
주 소 경기도 파주시 회동길 370(백산빌딩 3층)
전 화 02-914-1621(代)
팩 스 031-955-9911
이메일 edit@ibaeksan.kr
홈페이지 www.ibaeksan.kr

ISBN 978-89-7739-886-3 93740
값 18,000원